New Directions for Student Services

John H. Schuh
EDITOR-IN-CHIEF

Elizabeth J. Whitt
ASSOCIATE EDITOR

Managing Parent Partnerships:

Maximizing Influence, Minimizing Interference, and Focusing on Student Success

Karla C. Carney-Hall
EDITOR

Number 122 • Summer 2008
Jossey-Bass
San Francisco

MANAGING PARENT PARTNERSHIPS: MAXIMIZING INFLUENCE, MINIMIZING INTERFERENCE, AND FOCUSING ON STUDENT SUCCESS
Karla C. Carney-Hall (ed.)
New Directions for Student Services, no. 122
John H. Schuh, Editor-in-Chief
Elizabeth J. Whitt, Associate Editor

NEW DIRECTIONS FOR STUDENT SERVICES (ISSN 0164-7970, e-ISSN 1536-0695) is part of The Jossey-Bass Higher and Adult Education Series and is published quarterly by Wiley Subscription Services, Inc., A Wiley Company, at Jossey-Bass, 989 Market Street, San Francisco, California 94103-1741. Periodicals Postage Paid at San Francisco, California, and at additional mailing offices. POSTMASTER: Send address changes to New Directions for Student Services, Jossey-Bass, 989 Market Street, San Francisco, CA 94103-1741.

New Directions for Student Services is indexed in CIJE: Current Index to Journals in Education (ERIC), Contents Pages in Education (T&F), Current Abstracts (EBSCO), Education Index/Abstracts (H.W. Wilson), Educational Research Abstracts Online (T&F), ERIC Database (Education Resources Information Center), and Higher Education Abstracts (Claremont Graduate University).

Microfilm copies of issues and articles are available in 16mm and 35mm, as well as microfiche in 105mm, through University Microfilms Inc., 300 North Zeeb Road, Ann Arbor, Michigan 48106-1346.

SUBSCRIPTIONS cost $85 for individuals and $209 for institutions, agencies, and libraries in the United States. See ordering information page at end of book.

EDITORIAL CORRESPONDENCE should be sent to the Editor-in-Chief, John H. Schuh, N 243 Lagomarcino Hall, Iowa State University, Ames, Iowa 50011.

www.josseybass.com

CONTENTS

EDITOR'S NOTES

The past two decades demonstrated changes in relationships among parents, institutions, and students. In 1985 Cohen indicated that parents were not considered a viable constituent; however, by 2001 parent involvement on college and university campuses was increasing, inspiring another parent-focused issue for this series. Parents' roles as "consumers, adversaries, and partners" (Daniel and Scott, 2001) have not diminished in the past seven years; in fact, the media highlight the prevalence of "helicopter parents," who hover overhead, willing to advocate for their student at will, while college administrators respond with parent associations, parent services offices, web sites, listservs, and guest access to student records and electronic newsletters.

Although many administrators and faculty argue that the legal doctrine in loco parentis is back, others contend that our relationship with students is not that of a parent but a facilitator (Bickel and Lake, 1999) who focuses on educating and mentoring. In either event, colleges and university administrators wrestle with their commitment to the rights of students as independent adults, the new relationships between students and their parents, and parents who assert their influence as consumers.

The purpose of this volume is to assist administrators in understanding the impact of parental involvement on student development, in developing clear philosophies and complementary programs to assist parents, and in thinking critically about the many facets of campus life where parents may intervene—including fundraising, advocacy and crisis management, and potential legal implications. Parents affect many facets of higher education. In Chapter One, Karla C. Carney-Hall sets the stage for understanding the increase in parental involvement, the influence of parents, and implications for practice. In Chapter Two, Deborah J. Taub describes the impact of parent involvement on student development. Many administrators assume that parent involvement negatively impacts student autonomy development, identity development, and other types of critical development, as theorized by Chickering and Schlossberg. Instead, Taub presents research to both negate and support the assumption that parental involvement is negative.

Chapter Three builds on the concepts of student development to assist administrators in designing effective philosophies and messages for parents. Here Jerry Price explores broad philosophies and specific messages for diverse populations of parents, including first-generation parents and parents of color. Progressing from student development and appropriate frameworks for working with parents, Jeanine A. Ward-Roof, Patrick M. Heaton,

and Mary B. Coburn address programming for families in Chapter Four. Parent orientation and family weekends are explored, along with detailed information on web and print media outreach and parent associations. The primary purpose of programming for parents is to provide them with information and support. However, proactive programming does not address the reactive needs of parents when problems occur and crises emerge. In Chapter Five, Lynette S. Merriman describes the importance of administrators as advocates for students and parents in the face of crises and problems.

To address the needs of parents, many colleges and universities are establishing parent services offices and parent associations. In Chapter Six, Marjorie Savage outlines the process for developing, staffing, and assessing parent programs. Finally, administering an effective parent program includes a review of the legal relationship between students, parents, and the institution, as Thomas R. Baker shows in Chapter Seven.

Managing today's parents presents many opportunities and challenges. Parents are influential, highly invested in their student's success, and sometimes intrusive. This volume offers the best strategies to maximize their influence, minimize interference, and keep all energies focused on student success.

Karla C. Carney-Hall
Editor

References

Bickel, R. D., and Lake, P. *The Rights and Responsibilities of the Modern University.* Carolina Academic Press, 1999.

Cohen, R. D. (ed.). *Working with the Parents of College Students.* San Francisco: Jossey-Bass, 1985.

Daniel, B. V., and Scott, B. R. "Why Parents of Undergraduates Matter to Higher Education." In B. V. Daniel and B. R. Scott (eds.), *Consumers, Adversaries, and Partners: Working with Families of Undergraduates.* New Directions for Student Services, no. 94. San Francisco: Jossey-Bass, 2001.

KARLA C. CARNEY-HALL is vice president for student affairs at Hendrix College, Conway, Arkansas.

1

The overwhelming increase of parental involvement reported by today's college administrators requires a careful understanding of today's parents, their influence, and their expectations.

Understanding Current Trends in Family Involvement

Karla C. Carney-Hall

Parents of today's college students have much on their minds: paying for college, coping with their children's history of depression, ensuring safety, managing complex roommate relationships, and emphasizing academic success, to name just a few. Parental involvement has reportedly grown over the past few years, owing to many contributing factors: changing structures of families and campus environments, consumerism, and increased communication through technology (Merriman, 2007). The impact of parent involvement on student development is being studied with mixed results. In spite of both positive and negative implications of parent involvement, the media present unflattering characterizations of today's parents as "helicopter parents" hovering around the adult student prepared to intervene. Colleges' response to this increase in hovering varies, ranging from orientation bouncers to minimize involvement to parent associations and parent services offices to manage expectations and maximize influence. This chapter will provide an overview of current family trends, the influence and expectations of parents, and some preliminary implications as a framework for this volume as a whole.

Why Are Parents More Involved Now Than in the Past?

In *Consumers, Adversaries, and Partners: Working with the Families of Undergraduates,* Daniel and Scott (2001) identified parents as consumers, involved partners, and influential educators. Although parent involvement is not new,

NEW DIRECTIONS FOR STUDENT SERVICES, no. 122, Summer 2008 © Wiley Periodicals, Inc.
Published online in Wiley InterScience (www.interscience.wiley.com) • DOI: 10.1002/ss.271

their levels of involvement and expectations seem to be changing. In a 2006 national study of student affairs professionals at 127 institutions, 93 percent indicated an increase in interaction with parents in the last five years (Merriman, 2007).

Today's parents take a hands-on approach to managing their kids' lives, with particular attention to the details of educational experience (school activities, homework completion, assignments, and so on). The college admission and financial aid process encourages (and sometime requires) parent participation. Parents have been on campus tours, met with counselors, and have read all the preview materials, some targeting parents. Parents are emotionally invested in the college choice process.

Not only are families invested emotionally in the college choice process, they are also significantly invested financially. As consumers, they are partners in the financing of higher education, especially in light of shrinking public support for higher education funding. Even the process of applying for financial aid requires family tax and income information to calculate an expected family contribution, assuming that families will assist with college expenses (Kane, 1999). Because parents are paying more, they expect better service and higher quality programs and facilities. As higher education's high-paying customer, they will not hesitate to pursue the solution they want for any issue, no matter how minor. Consumer entitlement is turning today's parents into aggressive advocates. With expectations that parents contribute financially to rising college costs, it is no surprise that parents are interested consumers of education by being involved in the college experience.

Although parental involvement in the college experience is a logical extension of their financial commitment to higher education, their engaged partnership throughout their child's educational K–12 journey is increasingly encouraged by the federal government. Federal, state, and local governments have repeatedly emphasized the importance of parents in the educational process. The No Child Left Behind Act of 2001 listed parental involvement as one of six targeted areas, and schools receiving Title I funding must spend part of that funding on parent participation programs (Mattingly, Prislin, McKenzie, Rodrigues, and Kayzar, 2002). At the collegiate level, federal legislators recognized the importance of parents by extending the Family Educational Rights and Privacy Act (FERPA) to allow university officials to notify parents of underage students about alcohol violations in an effort to involve parents in students' decisions about drinking.

Parental involvement may also reflect the cultural environment of today's students discussed by Howe and Strauss (2000), who characterized today's parents as involved, overprotective, and child-focused. Part of this parenting style may stem from support systems at home. Family support systems are more diverse, with many students coming from divorced, blended, single-parent, or same-sex families. For example, since 1980 single-parent households have grown, with numbers of single custodial fathers growing to 3.1 million and never-married mothers growing to 7 million (Howe and Strauss, 2000). Family structures are particularly relevant to parents' roles as consumers. For example, divorced parents have lower incomes than married parents (Powers, 1997); however, they are still expected to financially support their child through college.

Parents may also be overprotective. Historical parent-child relationships, factors within the college environment, and the experience of students may be at the heart of these concerns. First, today's parents have always been protective of children, as evidenced by the prevalence of nanny cams, seatbelt laws, infant car seat regulations, bicycle helmets, and toy recalls. Second, today's students are racially, ethnically, and socioeconomically diverse (Coburn, 2006). Parents of color on predominantly white campuses find themselves feeling protective and seeking key administrators to ensure their students' success. Many students arrive with a history of mental health issues and learning disabilities for which their parents have actively advocated successfully with school administrators. Furthermore, incidents like the tragedy at Virginia Tech and Hurricane Katrina bring safety issues to the forefront. Finally, campus crime information is readily available through Cleary Act legislation. All these factors put safety at the forefront of parenting goals.

In addition to consumer mentality, federal encouragement, and changing family and campus environments, there is also the question of students' feelings about parental involvement. In fact, college students seem to welcome their parents to the collegiate process. College students themselves identify parents as the most influential people in their lives (Levine and Cureton, 1998). Students benefit from parent advocacy regarding everything from disability accommodation to roommate conflicts to mental health issues. Technology allows for continuous updates by cell phone, e-mail, or instant messaging. Parents are flooded with student-initiated communication that prompts engagement when issues arise.

What Is the Impact of Parental Involvement?

Parental involvement can potentially affect many components of the college experience: student development, institutional philosophies and policies, programs and services, and administrative structure. Unfortunately, anecdotal advice and opinions about parent relations dominate the higher education literature; research on the impact of parent involvement on college students is limited. Parents influence college choice (Toor, 2000) as well as a wide variety of cognitive and psychosocial developmental outcomes, including academic achievement (Wintre and Yaffe, 2000), university adjustment and retention (Boyd, Hunt, Hunt, Magoon, and VanBrunt, 1997; Wintre and Yaffe, 2000), alcohol decision making (Aziz and Shah, 1995; Deakin and Cohen, 1986; Reisberg, 2001), financing of higher education (Steelman and Powell, 1991, 1993), health issues (Birch and O'Toole, 1997; Lehr, Dilorio, Dudley, and Lipana, 2000), and career development (Silverman, 2000).

College Choice. If asked, admissions or financial aid counselors would likely report that parents are highly involved in the decision-making process. Not only do parents initiate conversations about college attendance, but they also attend campus visits, help complete applications for admissions and financial aid, and talk with advisors prior to a student even enrolling. In a study about the role of parents in financing and enrollment in higher education, Stringer, Cunningham, O'Brien, and Merisotis (1998) reported that 72 percent of parents helped complete admissions applications, 65 percent gave advice about schools, 57 percent spoke with an admissions counselor, 50 percent helped select the college or university, 83 percent helped complete financial aid forms, 80 percent obtained aid for their children, and 52 percent spoke with a financial aid counselor. Because parents are highly invested in the college choice process, one would expect that they also would continue their involvement with their college student.

Financial Support. Parents are also partners in the financial aspects of higher education. Sax, Astin, Korn, and Mahoney (1997) reported that 76 percent of all first-year college students receive parental financial assistance. Using national High School and Beyond survey data, Steelman and Powell (1991) reported that parents believed that they are primarily responsible for funding college, and their willingness to pay correlated with total income and number of other children. Parents also invested more in education when they received familial support themselves, suggesting continuity over generations (Steelman and Powell, 1991). Parental financial support is positively related to family income and educational attainment; in fact, Steelman and Powell (1993) found that parental income was among the most important influences of parental contribution to higher education. Stringer, Cunningham, O'Brien, and Merisotis (1998), however, added the cost of attendance at the institution as important to whether parents contribute to the cost of higher education. Overall, almost 50 percent of parents surveyed promised to pay all or most of their children's college expenses, and 42 percent promised to pay some of the expenses. Clearly, parents are significant contributors to the financial support of today's college students.

Because of increasing tuition costs, parents contribute more overall, but this amount covers a lower proportion of the average price of attendance; however, parents tended to save only 25 percent of the cost of attendance (Stringer, Cunningham, O'Brien, and Merisotis, 1998). Most parents failed to save early enough and were unrealistic about the cost of higher education (Stringer, Cunningham, O'Brien, and Merisotis, 1998). Consequently, more than 66 percent of parents offered a cash gift to their students to help meet educational expenses, and 10 percent reported taking out a personal loan (Stringer, Cunningham, O'Brien, and Merisotis, 1998).

Health and Wellness. Parents are also influential in health-related issues like alcohol decision making (Aziz and Shah, 1995; Deakin and Cohen, 1986; Reisberg, 2001), exercise, and wellness (Birch and O'Toole,

1997; Lehr, Dilorio, Dudley, and Lipana, 2000). For example, in a study conducted at Ohio State University (which surveyed 937 students), female college students were more likely to exercise with the support of family, whereas men tended to rely more heavily on the support of peers ("Encouraging College Students to Exercise," 2001).

Birch and O'Toole (1997) surveyed 269 traditional-age students at five public universities about student and parent health topics and guidelines for student-parent discussions. Sex, drugs, alcohol, and HIV/AIDS ranked as the most important health topics about which students were willing to and interested in discussing with their parents. Fifty-six percent of students surveyed thought conversations were important for their own health. Students recommended honesty, respect, trust, willingness to listen, and treating them like adults as important elements of those discussions.

In a survey of 732 college students about parent-student communication and safer sex behaviors, Lehr, Dilorio, Dudley, and Lipana (2000) found that race, sex, and parental communication were important factors influencing sexual activity. Female students reported higher levels of communication (both amount and openness) with mothers, whereas male students communicated with both parents equally. Comparing male and female students, men reported higher levels of openness with fathers. The relationship between parent communication and age of first sexual intercourse is curvilinear. For women, the most open and least open to communication with a parent were more likely to have initiated sex earlier.

In a study of parent and student behavior and attitudes about alcohol use and college, Deakin and Cohen (1986) reported that parents underestimated the amount of alcohol their children drank. Forty percent of the 403 parents surveyed allowed students to drink in their homes regardless of age. The likelihood of granting permission to drink at home increased with parental income. Parents in this study strongly believed that their sons and daughters were using good judgment in consuming alcohol. Parents supported campus alcohol restrictions, in spite of their permissiveness at home, and they preferred alcohol use to drug use for their children. Deakin and Cohen (1986) concluded that parents give mixed messages about alcohol use, especially related to the legal drinking age, tend to assume that problem drinkers are other people's children, and have an inaccurate perception of their children's alcohol use. Even though this study is relatively old, the issue of parent attitudes toward alcohol use is still pertinent to today's college students.

Student Development. Researchers studying college student adjustment have also explored the impact of parental attachment and autonomy development. Mattanah, Hancock, and Brand (2004) outlined researchers' early emphasis on the benefits of separation from parents for autonomy development, followed by the trend to support parental attachment as important for a healthy adjustment to college. Their study tested a model called individuation within relatedness where separation-individuation mediates secure attachment and college student adjustment (social, academic, and personal-emotional). They found that secure attachment with parents and separation-individuation was associated with positive college adjustment for both men and women. Additionally, male and female students viewed their attachment to their mothers as stronger than their attachment to their fathers and more important in their process of developing autonomy. Essentially this study supports the claim that positive attachment to parents helps facilitate autonomy development and social, academic, and personal-emotional adjustment.

What Do Parents Expect?

Although much advice is given about working with parents, very little research has been done about parental expectations. Parents often see themselves as the primary problem solvers for their children, so it is not surprising that they focus on concerns like health, safety, and discipline. Forbes (2001) indicated that parents expected to be notified of students' serious health issues, psychological problems, and campus policy violations.

Discipline and Safety. Because parents are often involved in students' judicial situations, Janosik (2001) studied parental perceptions of campus disciplinary systems. In comparing parent, student, and faculty attitudes about disciplinary procedures (in a group of 464 students), Janosik (2001) found that parents have high expectations for students' due process rights, including opportunities to meet with an advisor, the right to appeal, and a focus on educational outcomes. Because the outcomes of judicial processes can result in probation or suspension, the parental perspective is particularly important. With parental notification for alcohol offenses, colleges and university administrators have noted an increase in parental involvement in disciplinary matters.

Parental notification policies are criticized by some administrators for threatening the autonomy development of college students. However, others believe it necessary to ensure that families have accurate information about the student's disciplinary status.

Closely related to campus discipline is the issue of personal safety on campus. The Virginia Tech University tragedy involving a student gunman prompted many questions from parents across the country about crisis response and campus safety. Although parents recognize that students are responsible for their safety, parents have high expectations of college and university administrators for minimizing risk and communicating about safety concerns (Wills and Hines, 1994).

In a recent study of 435 parents' views on campus safety and the Cleary Act, which is designed to increase disclosure about safety issues, Janosik (2004) found that parent knowledge and use of the information contained in the Cleary Act is fairly low. Parents surveyed remembered campus crime as an issue presented during orientation (90 percent) and during admissions recruitment visits (70 percent). Eighty-four percent reported feeling more confident about those who were responsible for student safety after these conversations. As incidents of campus crime increase and receive more media attention, parental expectations regarding safety will grow.

Academics. Not only do parents express concern about campus safety and disciplinary matters, but they also expect to be involved in their children's academic experiences. In a study by Bers and Galowich (2002), focus groups with parents of traditional-aged community college students counted parental involvement with faculty and the academic experience among their top priorities.

College Outcomes. Parents are surveyed most frequently about the outcomes of a college education. Parents expect colleges and universities to focus on career development and job preparation (Bisset and others, 1999; Hersh, 1997; Turrentine, Schnure, Ostroth, and Ward-Roof, 2000) and personal and social development (Bisset and others, 1999; Child, Cooper, Hussell, and Webb, 1971). In a rare qualitative study of 1,382 parents, researchers identified job preparation, quality education, maturity and independence, graduation, enjoyment, academic success, and friendships and networks as parents' top-tier goals for the outcomes of a college education (Turrentine, Schnure, Ostroth and Ward-Roof, 2000). Ethnic diversity, graduate school preparation, a stimulating learning environment, health and safety, success and pride, citizenship preparation, social skill improvement, and faith development were low on parents' list of desired outcomes. In studying parental attitudes about liberal arts education, other researchers found that parents do not value the concept of learning for learning's sake (Child, Cooper, Hussell, and Webb, 1971; Hersh, 1997).

Implications

In today's college environment, parents have become a viable constituency that cannot be ignored. As with alumni, parents demonstrate significant investment in colleges and universities. Understanding the influence and expectations of parents allows college and university administrators to be more effective in partnering with them.

Parents Can Be Helpful. College and university administrators must remember that parents positively affect student success, whether providing valuable information about a student's mental health history or intervening with the student on alcohol choices. Given the unflattering media attention to helicopter parents, it is easy to conclude that all parent phone calls, e-mails, and visits are intrusive. However, parents are influential, their involvement is often welcomed by the student, and not all parental interaction is inappropriate.

Formal Institutional Philosophies Should Be Clearly Articulated. Parents will continue to be involved in college life. Given the financial investment, consumer mentality, and their encouraged involvement in the K–12 environment, parents will not shift their parenting approach without assistance from higher education professionals. Parents need to receive clear messages from each college or university: an overall institutional philosophy, clearly outlined paths to student success, the goals of student development (particularly autonomy development and self-advocacy), and specifics about college structure and resources.

Informal institutional philosophies about parents exist already on most campuses, but internal consistency is rare. For example, parents are told during the recruitment process that they are welcome to sit in on interviews, meet with academic advisors, or receive grades. However, the registrar's office may resist broad disclosure of information based on the Family Educational Rights to Privacy Act (FERPA). The residence life office states that students will be treated as adults and are expected to solve problems independently; however, when parents call the president's office about a roommate conflict, the staff are told to "fix it," regardless of campus policy or procedures. Professionals from the president to the admissions counselor need to be clear and consistent in the institution's approach to working with parents.

Messages to Parents Will Vary According to Institutional and Student Characteristics. Each institution will approach these messages differently. Messages will likely vary by institutional characteristics: public versus private institutions, two-year versus four-year institutions, traditional-age versus nontraditional-age student body, residential versus commuter institutions, and urban versus rural campuses. For example, small, private, traditional-aged, residential colleges will likely engage parents differently from urban, nonresidential, public universities. Because institutions prioritize issues differently, the approach to working with parents will vary.

Furthermore, the institutional philosophy on parents will vary by student characteristics, including gender, racial and ethnic diversity, disability, and others. Hispanic-serving institutions and historically Black institutions may find parental involvement that reflects family characteristics. Predominantly White institutions may see parents of color responding to the environment because of concerns about underrepresentation. Parents of female students may present different concerns from the parents of male students. Ironically, some campuses report greater involvement of parents of male students on parent advisory councils, in part due to the less frequent communication they receive directly from their sons.

Programming Should Facilitate Positive Relationships. Most college and university campuses provide programs for parents—parent orientation, family weekend, web sites, newsletters, and parent advisory boards or associations. Parents readily embrace their role as teachers, advocates, and information sources. Programs for parents should arm them with information to assist their children in accessing resources for success. In general, positive relationships with parents can mirror alumni relations. Parents, like alumni, can provide professional expertise on panels, social and financial capital access to others for fundraising or social networking, and can open their homes to prospective and current students in their area.

Parents Should Understand the Institution's Approach to Problem Solving and Crisis. Given their concerns about safety and judicial process, parents want to understand how best to access and provide information when a problem or crisis occurs. Concerns about safety are paramount, so crisis response protocols should include plans and guidelines for communication with parents, individually and collectively. For example, during an off-campus study trip where communication is limited, a guest faculty member dies. Should the college contact parents? Although all students are safe, parents may still have concerns, due to potential trauma and limited information. The driving question in crisis situations becomes whether outreach to parents is proactive or reactive.

Develop a Clear Point of Entry for Parents to Contact the Institution. Because parents will be involved, whether appropriately or inappropriately, institutions should develop a clear contact person for parents. Some institutions are developing parent services offices; others filter parents through the dean of students office. Regardless of the approach, identifying a primary entry point for parents will allow institutions to be consistent, responsive, and to identify the right personnel to respond to parents. Parent contact can be time-consuming and can require significant public relations skills. The designated parent contact should have both the time and the skill to be responsive. Parent newsletters, parent associations, orientation staff, and family weekend events can ensure that this person is a visible figure to parents. While establishing a parent liaison will be helpful to parents, it is also important that faculty and staff are comfortable talking with parents and referring appropriately. Providing professional development opportunities, talking about parent involvement in master's degree preparation programs, and reaching out to faculty who may be struggling with these interactions are equally important to ensuring that parent-institution interaction is handled appropriately. Clear communication, patience, empathy, and the ability to diffuse parental concerns are essential professional skills for staff working with parents.

Balance Student Privacy Rights with Parental Influence and Expectations. The concept of shared responsibility reflecting a partnership focused on the student's success is recommended to establish an appropriate balance. The idea that students, parents, and the institution are all partners in the process, each with a specific role, allows administrators to honor the influence of parents without relieving students of their adult responsibilities. By spelling out the boundaries of the institution's relationship with both parents and students, administrators can be clear about their legal responsibilities and philosophical expectations. Parents can better appreciate their interaction with the institution when they understand the importance of confidentiality as established by FERPA, parental notification of alcohol offenses, and the philosophical drawbacks of adults interceding to solve problems for students.

Students Need to Understand the New Relationship Too. Because students value parents' influence and involvement, students also have expectations about parental involvement. Many communicate with parents daily. Seniors welcome parental involvement in their job search so much that employers are developing parent information packets about their companies (Ray, 2007). Students may expect their parents to call the dean's office to resolve a problem or influence a judicial outcome. In essence, students defer to their parents by choice.

Unfortunately, institutional philosophy sometimes supports the empowerment of parents as problem solvers. In fact, one way to assess your institution's philosophy about parents is to ask students. If students perceive that parents "get things done" on campus, the institution is treating the parent as a customer and negating the commitment to the student as an adult problem solver. Although students are often told they are going to be treated as adults and must take responsibility for their choices, they may not fully understand what that means with respect to their parents.

Although students and institutions may encourage parent involvement, student affairs professionals must also convey a sense of student responsibility. What may seem obvious to student affairs professionals may not be so obvious to a new first-year student. On my campus one student ignored repeated reminders about immunization compliance; when she was removed from classes because of her health status, she apologized for not attending to this concern, stating that her mother told her she had already handled the situation. Students need to know that their parents will not be asked to respond to campus concerns.

References

Aziz, S., and Shah, A. A. "Home Environment and Peer Relations of Addicted and Non-addicted University Students." *The Journal of Psychology*, 1995, *129*(3), 277–284.

Bers, T. H., and Galowich, P. M. "Using Survey and Focus Group Research to Learn About Parents' Roles in the Community College Choice Process." *Community College Review*, 2002, *29*(4), 67–83.

Birch, D. A., and O'Toole, T. P. "Health Discussions between College Students and Parents: Results of a Delphi Study." *Journal of American College Health*, 1997, *46*(3), 139–144.

Bisset, J. D., and others. "Assessing the Importance of Educational Goals: A Comparison of Students, Parents, and Faculty." *Assessment & Evaluation in Higher Education*, 1999, *24*(4), 391–400.

Boyd, V. S., Hunt, P. F., Hunt, S. M., Magoon, T. M., and VanBrunt, J. E. "Parents as Referral Agents for their First-year College Students: A Retention Intervention." *Journal of College Student Development*, 1997, *38*(1), 191–192.

Child, D., Cooper, H. J., Hussell, C.G.I., and Webb, P. "Parents' Expectations of a University." *Universities Quarterly*, 1971, *25*(4), 484–490.

Coburn, K. "Organizing a Ground Crew for Today's Helicopter Parents." *About Campus,* 2006, *11*(3), 9–16.

Daniel, B. V., and Scott, B. R. "Why Parents of Undergraduates Matter to Higher Education." In B. V. Daniel and B. R. Scott (eds.), *Consumers, Adversaries, and Partners: Working with Families of Undergraduates.* New Directions for Student Services, no. 94. San Francisco: Jossey-Bass, 2001.

Deakin, S., and Cohen, E. "Alcohol Attitudes and Behaviors of Freshmen and Their Parents." *Journal of College Student Personnel,* 1986, *27*(6), 490–495.

"Encouraging College Students to Exercise: Ohio State University Study on Exercise Motivation and Habits." *USA Today* (magazine), Sept. 1, 2001.

Forbes, K. J. "Students and Their Parents: Where Do Campuses Fit In? *About Campus,* 2001, *6*(4), 11–17.

Hersh, R. H. "Intentions and Perceptions." *Change,* 1997, *29*(2), 16–24.

Howe, N., and Strauss, W. "Ground Zero of the Culture Wars (Family)." In N. Howe and W. Strauss (eds.), *Millennials Rising: The Next Great Generation.* New York: Vintage Books, 2000.

Janosik, S. M. "Expectations of Faculty, Parents, and Students for Due Process in Campus Disciplinary Hearings." *Journal of College Student Development,* 2001, *42*(2), 114–121.

Janosik, S. M. "Parents' Views on the Clery Act and Campus Safety." *Journal of College Student Development,* 2004, *45*(1), 43–56.

Jensen, L. A., Arnett, J. J., Feldman, S. S., and Cauffman, E. "The Right to Do Wrong: Lying to Parents Among Adolescents and Emerging Adults." *Journal of Youth and Adolescence,* 2004, *33*(2), 101–112.

Kane, T. J. *The Price of Admission: Rethinking How Americans Pay for College.* Washington, D.C.: Brookings Institution Press, 1999.

Lehr, S. T., DiIorio, C., Dudley, W. N., and Lipana, J. A. "The Relationship Between Parent-Adolescent Communication and Safer Sex Behaviors in College Students." *Journal of Family Nursing,* 2000, *6*(2), 180–196.

Levine, A., and Cureton, J. S. *When Hope and Fear Collide: A Portrait of Today's College Student.* San Francisco: Jossey-Bass, 1998.

Mattanah, J. F., Hancock, G. R., and Brand, B. L. "Parental Attachment, Separation-Individuation, and College Student Adjustment: A Structural Equation Analysis of Mediational Effects." *Journal of Counseling Psychology,* 2004, *51*(2), 213–225.

Mattingly, D., Prislin, R., McKenzie, T., Rodrigues, J., and Kayzar, B. "Evaluating Evaluations: The Case of Parent Involvement Programs." *Review of Educational Research,* 2002, *72*(4), 549–577.

Merriman, L. "Managing Parents 101: Minimizing Interference and Maximizing Good Will." *Leadership Exchange,* 2007, *5*(1), 14–19.

Powers, M. "The Hidden Costs of Divorce." *Human Ecology,* 1997, *25*(1), 4–8.

Ray, B. "Parents Who Hover." *The Cedar Rapids Gazette,* June 6, 2007, p. 1A.

Reisberg, L. "Two Years After College Started Calling Home, Administrators Say Alcohol Policy Works." *The Chronicle of Higher Education,* 2001, *49*(19), A34–A36.

Sax, L. J., Astin, A. W., Korn, W. S., and Mahoney, K. M. *The American Freshman: National Norms for Fall 1997.* Los Angeles: Higher Education Research Institute, 1997.

Silverman, R. E. "The Jungle: What's New in Recruitment and Pay. *Wall Street Journal,* Oct. 10, 2000, p. B4.

Steelman, L. C., and Powell, B. "Sponsoring the Next Generation: Parental Willingness to Pay for Higher Education." *American Journal of Sociology,* 1991, *96*(6), 1505–1529.

Steelman, L. C., and Powell, B. "Doing the Right Thing: Race and Parental Locus of Responsibility for Funding College." *Sociology of Education,* 1993, *66*(4), 223–243.

Stringer, W. L., Cunningham, A. F., O'Brien, C. T., and Merisotis, J. P. *It's All Relative: The Role of Parents in College Financing and Enrollment.* Indianapolis, Ind.: USA Group Foundation, 1998.

Toor, R. "Pushing Parents and Other Tales of the Admissions Game." *The Chronicle of Higher Education,* 2000, *47*(6), B18.

Turrentine, C. G., Schnure, S. L., Ostroth, D. D., and Ward-Roof, J. A. "The Parent Project: What Parents Want from the College Experience." *NASPA Journal,* 2000, *38*(1), 31–43.

Wills, S. B., and Hines, E. R. "Perceptions of Residence Hall Security." *Journal of College Student Development,* 1994, *35,* 488–489.

Wintre, M. G., and Yaffe, M. "First-year Students' Adjustment to University Life as a Function of Relationships with Parents." *Journal of Adolescent Research,* 2000, *15*(1), 9–38.

KARLA C. CARNEY-HALL *is the vice president for student affairs at Hendrix College, Conway, Arkansas.*

2

This chapter considers the impact that parental involvement may have on the psychosocial development of college students.

Exploring the Impact of Parental Involvement on Student Development

Deborah J. Taub

College student development theory in general has had little to say about the parents of college students. This fact reflects the era in which student development theory arose: the late 1960s and early 1970s. The *Dixon* v. *Alabama* decision, which is regarded as implicitly rejecting the doctrine of in loco parentis, was handed down in 1961, and the 26th Amendment to the U.S. Constitution, which lowered the age of majority for voting to eighteen, was ratified a decade later in 1971 (Nuss, 2003). The student affairs profession embraced student development theory as a new foundation for the profession at the same time that it embraced the new concept of the college student as adult. This progression seemed to leave little room for a role for parents when students were to be viewed as adults. In fact, in 1985 Cohen observed that "we do not consider parents part of our client population" (Cohen, 1985b, p. 3) and that "the concerns of our students' parents are marginal in our day-to-day work" (Cohen, 1985a, p. 1).

However, today we cannot so easily dismiss the parents of college students as marginal to our daily work. The current generation of college students—the Millennial Generation (Howe and Strauss, 2000, 2003)—is described as being extremely close with their parents. The 1997 Gallup Youth Survey (as cited in Howe and Strauss, 2003) reported that 90 percent of young people considered themselves to be very close to their parents. According to a recent Pew Research Center report (Kohut and others, 2007), approximately 80 percent of eighteen- to twenty-five-year-olds said that they had talked to their parents in the past day. Another recent study found that first-year college

NEW DIRECTIONS FOR STUDENT SERVICES, no. 122, Summer 2008 © Wiley Periodicals, Inc.
Published online in Wiley InterScience (www.interscience.wiley.com) • DOI: 10.1002/ss.272

15

students communicated with their parents an average of 10.41 times per week, with most of that communication being initiated by parents (Grace, 2006).

For their part, the parents of today's traditional-age college students are close with their children and actively involved in their children's college experience (Coburn, 2006; College Parents of America, 2007a, 2007b; Daniel, Evans, and Scott, 2001; Howe and Strauss, 2003). The term that has been coined to describe these parents—helicopter parents—reflects their defining tendency to bring their children to campus, but to continue to hover, ready to swoop in if needed (Howe and Strauss, 2003). These parents have been involved with their children's lives throughout their childhoods (remember the "soccer moms" of the 1990s) and clearly expect to continue this involvement into the college years (College Parents of America, 2007b; Scott and Daniel, 2001). Student affairs professionals have noticed this increasing involvement, not always with pleasure (Forbes, 2001).

The term "helicopter parents" has proven to be popular, yielding over 1.99 million hits on Google as of October 17, 2007, probably because its graphic imagery captures something that people recognize as true. However, the label also obscures a portion of reality as well. The term "helicopter parents" focuses attention solely on the parents, distracting the speaker and the listener from the fact that today's students are equal partners in the phenomenon, frequently initiating contact and calling upon their parents for assistance.

Given the increasing closeness and contact between college students and their parents, it is time to examine how this close relationship with parents might affect student development. This chapter will focus primarily on aspects of students' psychosocial development and will, where possible, draw on findings from research.

Psychosocial Theory

Psychosocial developmental theory is concerned with the content or tasks of development. Generally speaking, psychosocial theories arrange these tasks in a series of stages, often chronological. The stages come about as the result of the combination of factors internal to the individual (such as physical and cognitive maturity) and the demands, expectations, and pressures of society. Psychosocial theories are therefore theories about development in the context of the environment. Because external expectations and pressures are included, psychosocial development is a particularly important area to examine when discussing the role and impact of parents on college student development. Examples of psychosocial theories that address college students include those of Erikson (1959, 1968), Chickering (1969; Chickering and Reisser, 1993), Arnett (2000, 2004), Schlossberg, Waters, and Goodman (1995), Evans, Forney, and Guido-DiBrito (1998), and Knefelkamp, Widick, and Parker (1978). In this chapter I will use the theoretical frameworks provided by Chickering's model and Schlossberg's transition theory to consider the effect of parental involvement on college students' development.

Chickering's Theory. Arguably the most well-known and widely used psychosocial theory of college student development is that of Chickering (1969; Chickering and Reisser, 1993). Chickering built on the work of Erikson (1959, 1968), who identified the establishment of identity as the central developmental task of the college years. Chickering (1969) believed that the concept of identity was too abstract to provide guidance for practice to those who work with college students; he developed his model to provide greater specificity and concreteness to the developmental task of establishing identity. Chickering and Reisser (1993) identified seven psychosocial tasks (called "vectors") of the college years that compose the overarching task of identity development. Typically, students in the first two college years are expected to be dealing with the vectors of developing competence, managing emotions, moving through autonomy toward interdependence, and developing mature interpersonal relationships, whereas the later vectors are most likely to be in the forefront of juniors' and seniors' development. Of the seven vectors, those most relevant to this discussion are the vectors of developing competence, moving through autonomy toward interdependence, developing identity, developing purpose, and developing integrity.

Developing Competence. The vector of developing competence focuses on development of basic skills in the intellectual, interpersonal, and physical and manual arenas. Development of competence in these three arenas leads to the development of an overall sense of competence: a sense that one can cope with what comes up. This self-confidence serves as a base for taking risks required for additional growth and development.

"Helicopter parents" are criticized by professionals in higher education for swooping in to try to solve all of their college students' problems—whether those problems are roommate conflicts, grade disputes, or conduct issues. Such behavior can interfere with students' development of competence in two major ways. First, when parents tackle challenges instead of allowing students to do so, the students are deprived of the experiences by which they would develop intellectual, interpersonal, and physical and manual competence. It is only through struggling with challenges in these areas that the competencies can be developed. Second, students' development of a sense of competence is impaired, not only by depriving them of the opportunities to develop competence in one or more areas but also by communicating to the student through these actions that the parents believe that the student is not competent to solve problems on his or her own. Conversely, parents can contribute to students' development of competence by allowing them the opportunity to try solving problems on their own and by communicating confidence that they are capable of solving the problem. Parents have the option to step in to assist the student and provide support if the problem proves to be too great for him or her to solve.

NEW DIRECTIONS FOR STUDENT SERVICES • DOI: 10.1002/ss

The research on the impact of parents on the development of competence is limited and mixed. This research has focused on the development of social or interpersonal competence. Although a study by Bartle-Haring and Sabatelli (1997) suggested that lack of differentiation from parents is related to lower interpersonal competence in undergraduates, other research (Bell and others, 1985; Kenny, 1987a, 1987b; Kenny and Donaldson, 1991) suggested that attachment to parents is related to social competence in first-year college students.

It appears that healthy attachment to parents can support students' development of social and interpersonal competence. However, college students need opportunities to address challenges in the areas of social and interpersonal competence, intellectual competence, and physical and manual competence in order to develop competencies in these specific areas and a resulting sense of overall competence. Following the wisdom of Sanford (1962), students need to experience a balance between challenge and support so that they can develop and move forward. Excessive support from parents can inhibit development of competence. More studies are needed to explore the impact of increasing parental involvement on students' development in all facets of competence.

Moving Through Autonomy Toward Interdependence. The vector "moving through autonomy toward interdependence" has three major components: emotional independence, instrumental independence, and the recognition of interdependence. Emotional independence involves freedom from the need for continual reassurance and support, and instrumental independence involves the ability to carry out activities and solve problems independently and to be mobile in relation to one's needs. In the second edition of *Education and Identity* (1993), Chickering and Reisser noted that this vector, which had previously been called "developing autonomy" (Chickering, 1969), had been renamed to give greater prominence to the culmination of the vector in interdependence. The recognition of interdependence is a mature acceptance that neither total dependence nor total independence is ideal.

It is arguably in the vector of moving through autonomy toward interdependence that student affairs professionals have the most concerns about the impact of parental involvement on students' development. In this vector Chickering (1969; Chickering and Reisser, 1993) described the process of the development of emotional autonomy as beginning with a disengagement from the parents, moving to reliance on peers and nonparental adults, and finally to independence from those persons as well. Chickering and Reisser explicitly described how parents could inhibit students' development of autonomy by being overly restrictive, unsupportive, or domineering. Taub (1995) found that parents' provision of emotional support was inversely related to college women's development of autonomy; in other words, parents providing excessive emotional support can inhibit students' development of autonomy. Chickering and Reisser also explained that parents can help students develop emotional autonomy by providing them with opportunities to make choices before college. Perhaps reflecting their ideas that the development of emotional autonomy begins with disengagement from the parents and that parents' actions can inhibit emotional autonomy development, Chickering and Reisser do not address the idea of how parents can help students develop emotional autonomy once students are in college.

The second component of this vector, instrumental independence, concerns the ability to solve problems on one's own and the ability to go where one needs to go to access the resources to meet one's needs. Chickering and Reisser (1993) described emotional independence and instrumental independence as inextricably linked. If students lack opportunities to solve problems on their own, they may have difficulty achieving separation from their parents; if they rely on their parents for continual feedback and reassurance, they may be reluctant to attempt to solve their problems independently.

Researchers have explored the idea of college students experiencing a break from their parents as described by Chickering (1969; Chickering and Reisser, 1993). Kenny (1990), Rice (1992), and Taub (1997), for instance, found considerable stability in the levels of students' attachment to parents across the college years. Arnett (2000) terms the developmental period of the late teens through the twenties "emerging adulthood" and describes it as a time of "semiautonomy" (Goldscheider and Davanzo, 1986), when young adults may live separately from their parents (as in a residence hall or an off-campus apartment) but are still dependent on their parents in important ways. Arnett (2007) challenged the popular belief that this generation of young people simply does not want to grow up; he cited a variety of social reasons for the longer time it takes these days to grow up. Goldscheider and Davanzo considered semiautonomy to be an "intermediate step" on the road to adulthood (p. 200).

Kenny and Rice (1995) described attachment to parents—rather than a break from parents—as providing a secure base that supports the development of autonomy. Taub (1997) found that although college women's level of attachment to parents across class years was stable, their level of autonomy increased from first year to senior year. Sullivan and Sullivan (1980) found that college men who lived on campus both maintained close emotional ties to parents and developed independence.

It appears that students can develop autonomy without experiencing the break from parents described in Chickering's theory and that their attachment to parents actually may aid them in their autonomy development. If so, the frequent contact between students and their parents (College Parents of America, 2007a; Grace, 2006; Kohut and others, 2007) is not in and of itself a cause for concern for student development. It is only when students are unable or unwilling to attempt to solve problems on their own that there may be cause for concern about their development of emotional and instrumental autonomy.

Developing Identity. As he built on the work of Erikson (1968), Chickering (1969; Chickering and Reisser, 1993) identified the task of identity formation as the central developmental task of the traditional college years. Chickering and Reisser (1993) described several different components comprising the developing identity vector: comfort with body and appearance, comfort with gender and sexual orientation, sense of one's social and cultural identity, clarification of self-concept through roles, sense of self in response to feedback from others, self-acceptance, self-esteem, and stability and integration. They have little to say about the role of parents in these components of identity development.

Parents logically would play a role in the development of sense of self in response to feedback from valued others. The family is considered to serve as an important reference group for young people (Caplan, 1982), providing feedback on attitudes and behavior. The family also is seen as the source of many of the components that form an individual's identity (Caplan, 1982).

Family certainly plays a role in students' social and cultural identity development (Cross, 1991; Parham, 1993). Tatum (1997) pointed out that connecting with Black peers plays an important role in the development of Black racial identity development. According to Tatum, Black adolescents typically turn from the role models offered by adult family members to their own peers to find support and answers about how to "be Black." No teenager, she pointed out, wants to be like his or her parents. However, in the case of Black adolescents growing up in predominantly White neighborhoods, Black peers are more scarce. Tatum identified the need in these situations for active parental involvement to provide opportunities for their teenagers to interact with Black peers through social structures such as Black churches and social organizations.

Parents' attitudes and actions can be particularly important to multiracial young people's cultural identity development (Root, 1996). Multiracial young people may choose to identify with the race of one parent or the other, or they may choose to identify themselves as multiracial (Thornton, 1996). Their choices may be different from the way their parents have identified them, which might be difficult for parents to accept and support. However, parental support in discussing these issues and choices is important for the identity development of multiracial individuals (Root, 1996).

Sexual orientation identity development has been compared to the cultural identity development process of people of color (Rotheram-Borus and Fernandez, 1995). Parents can be important in the sexual orientation identity development of gay, lesbian, bisexual, and transgender (GLBT) students and their development of comfort with their sexual orientation. Coming out to significant others, such as family members, is seen as one of the most difficult, and the most important, developmental tasks for GLBT individuals (Ben-Ari, 1995). GLBT individuals are concerned and even fearful about coming out to parents (Ben-Ari, 1995; Mosher, 2001). One of the primary fears is the possibility of being rejected by parents (Ben-Ari, 1995). A positive reception from parents to their child's coming out is associated with positive identity development and with self-esteem (Ben-Ari, 1995; Carrion and Lock, 1997).

Arnett (2000, 2004) considers identity exploration to be the central feature of emerging adulthood. Erikson (1968) and Chickering (1969; Chickering and Reisser, 1993) believed that separation and individuation were necessary for successful identity formation. However, researchers have begun questioning that belief. Identify formation is believed to be influenced more by attachment relationships than by individuation (Samuolis, Layburn, and Schiaffino, 2001). Attachment to parents is seen as providing a secure base for identity development (Kenny, 1987b; Kenny and Rice, 1995). Identity achievement in college women was found to be positively associated with parental attachment (Schultheiss and Blustein, 1994a). In another study, college students' identity achievement was supported by a secure base via attachment to their mothers, but fathers' anxieties about separation inhibited women college students' identity development (Bartle-Haring, Brucker, and Hock, 2002).

Developing Purpose. Chickering and Reisser (1993) describe the process of developing purpose as formulating plans that integrate one's vocational aspirations, family commitments, and personal interests. Although Chickering and Reisser have little to say about the role of parents in students' development of purpose, the influence of parents on college students' career development is well documented in the literature. Parents influence students' career choices (Fisher and Padmawidjaja, 1999; Young and Friesen, 1992), and they help students develop career plans (Kenny, 1990). In a study of parents of college students, 14 percent reported being asked frequently or very frequently by their students for advice and assistance in academic matters, some of those presumably around major selection. In the same study, 37 percent of responding parents reported having extreme or great concern about their students' academics and 31 percent reported extreme or great concern about their students' career planning (College Parents of America, 2007a).

Parents influence students' tendencies toward decisiveness or indecision (Ferrari and Olivette, 1993). Schultheiss and Blustein (1994b) found that college women's (but not men's) development of purpose was related to parental attachment. Ketterson and Blustein (1997) found that parental attachment supported students' career exploration. Parents also influence the ways in which students intend to balance family and career (Kerpelman and Schvaneveldt, 1999).

However, recent reports suggest that today's generation of parents may be going beyond encouragement and support of their college-age children's career plans and aspirations (Armour, 2007; Irvine, 2006; Shellenbarger, 2006). There are reports of parents attending career fairs with their students, contacting potential employers, accompanying students to job interviews, negotiating offers with employers, and discussing their recently employed students' performance reviews with employers. Such extensive involvement by parents can interfere not only with students' development of competence and autonomy but also with their development of purpose. In situations such as these, it would appear that the student is not so much developing a life plan as complying with a plan developed and pursued by the parent. It is in activities such as these that parental involvement moves beyond support of students' development to a force that interferes with that development. Studies that move beyond anecdotal accounts to examine the true extent of parental involvement in students' career development and early career stages and the effect of that involvement on students' development of purpose and career maturity are needed.

Developing Integrity. The vector of developing integrity has to do with one's core values and beliefs. For Chickering and Reisser (1993) this vector involves moving from a rigid application of beliefs to a more nuanced and flexible application, affirming which values and beliefs one is going to use as a guide and bringing one's behavior into congruence with those values and beliefs. Not surprisingly, Chickering and Reisser (1993) reflect that parents are one of the key sources of the values and beliefs that students bring to college. They also acknowledge that developing congruence between beliefs and behaviors sometimes can cause conflicts between students and their parents. The process of developing integrity may lead students ultimately to choose to embrace the values and beliefs of their parents, but the process also may lead to a rejection of those values and beliefs.

A study of African American college students (Constantine, Miville, Warren, Gainor, and Lewis-Coles, 2006) found that parents played an important role in the development of the students' religious and spiritual beliefs and behaviors. Some participants reported negative reactions from parents when they moved away from adherence to their parents' beliefs and behaviors; they later returned on their own to these beliefs. Another study (Richards, 1991) found that religiously committed students exhibited less separation from parents than other participants.

Today's Millennial students have been described as more conventional than previous generations (Howe and Strauss, 2000, 2003). They are more likely to identify with their parents and to share their values. They may thus be less willing to explore the values and beliefs they bring to college and may instead be more inclined to foreclose, accepting those beliefs without question or exploration (Marcia, 1966, 1980). It also is possible that those Millennial students who do explore their values and beliefs may be reluctant to adopt values and beliefs that are different from those of their parents, because they describe themselves as being extremely close to their parents (Howe and Strauss, 2000, 2003). Courses and other experiences (such as service-learning projects) that require students to explore issues of values and belief may be particularly challenging to students and also could be seen as threatening by parents.

Schlossberg's Transition Theory. Although Schlossberg's transition theory (Schlossberg, Waters, and Goodman, 1995) is not a stage theory, Evans, Forney, and Guido-DiBrito (1998) classified it as a psychosocial theory, largely because of its focus on development across the life span. As with other psychosocial theories, transition theory takes into account the con-

NEW DIRECTIONS FOR STUDENT SERVICES • DOI: 10.1002/ss

text in which development occurs and is focused on the content of development. The focus of the theory is people's ability to cope with transitions. The theory describes the sets of factors that influence individuals' ability to cope with transition. These sets of factors, called the Four Ss, are labeled as situation, self, strategies, and support. Situation factors are those that describe the transition situation, such as the timing, the duration, concurrent stress, and the individual's previous experience with similar transitions. Self factors are those that describe the individual, both in terms of demographic characteristics (age, gender, race or ethnicity, and so on) and of psychological resources (such as optimism and self-efficacy). Strategies refer to the things that the individual does to cope with a transition. Support refers to the people and the institutions to which the individual in transition can turn for help.

Sources of support help the person in transition in a number of ways. They can share tasks, helping the individual take care of business. They can provide emotional support in the form of comfort, reassurance, and encouragement. They can provide advice. They may help in material or tangible ways such as money or other material offerings. They also can provide honest feedback to the individual in transition. In transition theory, parents are seen as a potential source of support for the student in transition.

The transition to college can be a time of upheaval for first-year students, as they leave much of what they have known for something relatively unknown (Benjamin, Earnest, Gruenewald, and Arthur, 2007). Greene (1998) described first-year students as experiencing the highest levels of distress of all college students. They are confronted with an extraordinary number of choices and decisions—about course selections, living arrangements, organizations, and majors—that can lead to feelings of being pressured and overwhelmed (Coburn, 2006).

Parents can serve as an important source of support to the student transitioning to college. They may do so in any of the ways described by Schlossberg and her colleagues. In their frequent contact with their students (College Parents of America, 2007a; Grace, 2006; Kohut and others, 2007), parents can provide reassurance, comfort, and support, as well as advice and honest feedback. Parents also provide material help in the form of financial support or other tangible support.

Furthermore, parents can and do provide these types of support to their students beyond the first year of college as students make other transitions—from one major to another, to and from study abroad, co-op, or internship, from one institution to another, graduation, and so on. In one recent study (College Parents of America, 2007a), it was found that 33 percent of responding parents of college students frequently or very frequently provided their college students with advice or assistance about financial matters, 14 percent about academics, and 14 percent on health and safety. It is important to note that this advice or assistance was provided at the request of the student. Even greater percentages of prospective college parents (parents of students who were college-bound) anticipated being asked for advice and assistance in these areas (College Parents of America, 2007b). Sixty-four percent of Millennial-age young people were most likely to choose their families as the people they would turn to for advice about a serious problem (Kohut and others, 2007). Almost 75 percent of them reported receiving financial help from their parents in the past year; 64 percent reported that parents helped them complete tasks such as errands and housework (Kohut and others, 2007).

These types of supportive activities—sharing tasks and burdens, offering advice, and providing emotional, psychological, and material support—are frequently cited when labeling parents as "helicopter parents." The primary concern is that these activities may impede the development of the student.

However, some research suggests that parental support can be helpful to students in adjusting to college. For example, Lapsley, Rice, and FitzGerald (1990) found that attachment to parents predicted academic adjustment and personal-emotional adjustment in first-year college students; they further found that upper-class students' attachment to parents predicted social adjustment as well as academic and personal-emotional adjustment. This research is consistent with the view of support in transition theory. It also is consistent with Sanford's (1962) view that, in the appropriate amount, support in the face of challenge can facilitate rather than impede development.

Conclusion

High levels of parental involvement in the lives of today's college students and increased contact and communication between today's college students and their parents has caused concern for some in higher education (Coburn, 2006; Forbes, 2001). Among the concerns is the potential for adverse impact on students' development. However, parental involvement is not necessarily detrimental to students' development and may in fact be supportive of development in some areas. As always, a delicate balance of challenge and support (Sanford, 1962) is the best formula for promoting student development.

Student affairs professionals can help by finding ways to educate parents about how best to support students without oversupporting them. Following are some ideas to keep in mind for coaching parents.

1. They are invested in being good parents. These parents very likely have read the child-rearing books of the 1990s covering how best to be good parents. They are therefore highly motivated and open to coaching about what good parenting to college students looks like. After all, when they sent their students off to preschool, they learned that hovering communicated

two things: that there's something to be scared of and that Mom or Dad doesn't think you can handle it. That same lesson just needs to be reactivated for the college setting.

2. Parents and higher education professionals share the goals of student success and student growth and maturity. Clearly articulating to parents that we share these goals communicates understanding to parents and sets a tone of partnership rather than one of opposition.

3. Teaching them a little about student development can be helpful. Because today's parents are invested in being good parents and are open to learning, they may be interested to learn some basic student development theory. Not only does this normalize for parents what they will be experiencing with their students, but it also establishes a "common language" for communicating about students (Knefelkamp, 1980, p. 17). The language of student development theory can make it easier to explain to parents how to be partners in students' development of emotional and instrumental independence, purpose, and integrity.

4. Acknowledge explicitly that parents have a role. Research supports the idea that parental support and involvement can be helpful to students' development. In messages to parents, it is important to recognize and honor them for this role.

References

Armour, S. "'Helicopter' Parents Hover When Kids Job Hunt." *USA Today*, April 23, 2007. Retrieved March 12, 2008, from www.usatoday/money/economy/employment/2007-04-23-helicopter-parents-usat_N.htm.

Arnett, J. J. "Emerging Adulthood: A Theory of Development from the Late Teens Through the Twenties." *American Psychologist*, 2000, 55, 469–480.

Arnett, J. J. *Emerging Adulthood: The Winding Road from the Late Teens Through the Twenties.* New York: Oxford University Press, 2004.

Arnett, J. J. "Suffering, Selfish, Slackers? Myths and Realities About Emerging Adults." *Journal of Youth and Adolescence*, 2007, 36, 23–29.

Bartle-Haring, S., Brucker, P., and Hock, E. "The Impact of Parental Separation Anxiety on Identity Development in Late Adolescence and Early Adulthood." *Journal of Adolescent Research*, 2002, 17, 439–450.

Bartle-Haring, S., and Sabatelli, R. M. "Emotional Reactivity Towards Parents and Interpersonal Competence: Differences Across Gender and Type of Relationship." *Journal of Youth and Adolescence*, 1997, 26, 399–413.

Bell, N., and others. "Family Relationships and Social Competence During Late Adolescence." *Journal of Youth and Adolescence*, 1985, 14, 109–119.

Ben-Ari, A. "The Discovery That an Offspring Is Gay: Parents', Gay Men's, and Lesbians' Perspectives." *Journal of Homosexuality*, 1995, 30, 89–112.

Benjamin, M., Earnest, K., Gruenewald, D., and Arthur, G. "The First Weeks of the First Year." In E. L. Moore (ed.), *Student Affairs Staff as Teachers.* San Francisco: Jossey-Bass, 2007.

Caplan, G. "The Family as a Support System." In H. I. McCubbin, A. E. Cauble, and J. M. Patterson (eds.), *Family Stress, Coping, and Social Support.* Springfield, Ill.: Charles C. Thomas, 1982.

Carrion, V. G., and Lock, J. "The Coming Out Process: Developmental Stages for Sexual Minority Youth." *Clinical Child Psychology and Psychiatry,* 1997, *2,* 369–377.

Chickering, A. W. *Education and Identity.* San Francisco: Jossey-Bass, 1969.

Chickering, A. W., and Reisser, L. *Education and Identity.* (2nd ed.) San Francisco: Jossey-Bass, 1993.

Coburn, K. L. "Organizing a Ground Crew for Today's Helicopter Parents." *About Campus,* July/Aug. 2006, pp. 9–16.

Cohen, R. D. "Editor's Notes." In R. D. Cohen (ed.), *Working with the Parents of College Students.* San Francisco: Jossey-Bass, 1985a.

Cohen, R. D. "From in Loco Parentis to Auxilio Parentum." In R. D. Cohen (ed.), *Working with the Parents of College Students.* San Francisco: Jossey-Bass, 1985b.

College Parents of America. "Second Annual National Survey on College Parent Experiences." 2007a. Retrieved May 21, 2007, from www.collegeparents.org/files/2007-Current-Parent-Survey-Summary.pdf.

College Parents of America. "Second Annual National Survey on Future College Parent Expectations." 2007b. Retrieved May 21, 2007, from www.collegeparents.org/files/2007-Future-Parent-Survey.pdf.

Constantine, M. G., Miville, M. L., Warren, A. K., Gainor, K. A., and Lewis-Coles, M.E.L. "Religion, Spirituality, and Career Development in African American College Students: A Qualitative Inquiry." *The Career Development Quarterly,* 2006, *54,* 227–241.

Cross, W. E. *Shades of Black: Diversity in African American Identity.* Philadelphia: Temple University Press, 1991.

Daniel, B. V., Evans, S. G., and Scott, B. R. "Understanding Family Involvement in the College Experience Today." In B. V. Daniel and B. R. Scott (eds.), *Consumers, Adversaries, and Partners: Working with the Families of Undergraduates.* San Francisco: Jossey-Bass, 2001.

Erikson, E. H. *Identity and the Life Cycle.* New York: Norton, 1959.

Erikson, E. H. *Identity: Youth and Crisis.* New York: Norton, 1968.

Evans, N. J., Forney, D. S., and Guido-DiBrito, F. *Student Development in College: Theory, Research, and Practice.* San Francisco: Jossey-Bass, 1998.

Ferrari, J. R., and Olivette, M. J. "Perceptions of Parental Control and the Development of Indecision Among Late Adolescent Females." *Adolescence,* 1993, *28,* 963–970.

Fisher, T. A., and Padmawidjaja, I. "Parental Influences on Career Development Perceived by African American and Mexican American College Students." *Journal of Multicultural Counseling and Development,* 1999, *27,* 136–153.

Forbes, K. J. "Students and Their Parents: Where Do Campuses Fit In?" *About Campus,* Sept./Oct. 2001, pp. 11–17.

Goldscheider, F. K., and Davanzo, J. "Semiautonomy and Leaving Home During Early Adulthood." *Social Forces,* 1986, *65,* 187–201.

Grace, C. O. "Family Ties." *Middlebury Magazine.* Fall 2006. Retrieved March 12, 2008, from http://www.middlebury.edu/administration/middmag/archive/2006/fall/features/family_ties/.

Greene, H. R. *The Select: Realities of Life and Learning in America's Elite Colleges.* New York: HarperCollins, 1988.

Howe, N., and Strauss, W. *Millennials Rising: The Next Great Generation.* New York: Vintage Books, 2000.

Howe, N., and Strauss, W. *Millennials Go to College.* Washington, D.C.: American Association of Collegiate Registrars and Admissions Officers, 2003.

Irvine, M. "'Helicopter' Parents Try Too Hard." *The Boston Globe,* November 7, 2006. Retrieved March 12, 2008, from http://www.boston.com/news/nation/articles/2006/11/07/helicopter_parents_try_too_hard/?page=1.

Kenny, M. "The Extent and Function of Parental Attachment Among First-Year College Students." *Journal of Youth and Adolescence,* 1987a, *16,* 17–27.

Kenny, M. "Family Ties and Leaving Home for College: Recent Findings and Implications." *Journal of College Student Personnel,* 1987b, *xx,* 438–442.

Kenny, M. "College Seniors' Perceptions of Parental Attachments: The Value and Stability of Family Ties." *Journal of College Student Development,* 1990, *31,* 39–46.

Kenny, M. E., and Donaldson, G. A. "Contributions of Parental Attachment and Family Structure to the Social and Psychological Functioning of First-Year College Students." *Journal of Counseling Psychology,* 1991, *38,* 479–486.

Kenny, M. E., and Rice, K. G. "Attachment to Parents and Adjustment in Late Adolescent College Students: Current Status, Applications, and Future Considerations." *The Counseling Psychologist,* 1995, *23,* 433–456.

Kerpelman, J. L., and Schvaneveldt, P. L. "Young Adults' Anticipated Identity Importance of Career, Marital, and Parental Roles: Comparisons of Men and Women with Different Role Balance Orientations." *Sex Roles,* 1999, *41,* 189–216.

Ketterson, T. U., and Blustein, D. L. "Attachment Relationships and the Career Exploration Process." *The Career Development Quarterly,* 1997, *46,* 167–178.

Knefelkamp, L., Widick, C., and Parker, C. A. *Applying New Developmental Findings.* New Directions for Student Services, no. 4. San Francisco: Jossey-Bass, 1978.

Knefelkamp, L. L. "Faculty and Student Development in the '80s: Renewing the Community of Scholars." *Current Issues in Higher Education,* no. 5. Washington, D.C.: American Association for Higher Education, 1980.

Kohut, A., and others. *How Young People View Their Lives, Futures, and Politics: A Portrait of "Generation Next."* Washington, D.C.: Pew Research Center for the People and the Press, 2007. Retrieved May 21, 2007, from http://people-press.org/reports/display.php3?ReportID=300.

Lapsley, D. K., Rice, K. G., and FitzGerald, D. P. "Adolescent Attachment, Identity, and Adjustment to College: Implications for the Continuity of Adaptation Hypothesis." *Journal of Counseling and Development,* 1990, *68,* 561–565.

Marcia, J. E. "Development and Validation of Ego-Identity Status." *Journal of Personality and Social Psychology,* 1966, *3,* 551–558.

Marcia, J. E. "Identity in Adolescence." In J. Adelson (ed.), *Handbook of Adolescent Psychology.* New York: Wiley, 1980.

Mosher, C. M. "The Social Implications of Sexual Identity Formation and the Coming-Out Process: A Review of the Theoretical and Empirical Literature." *The Family Journal,* 2001, *9,* 164–173.

Nuss, E. M. "The Development of Student Affairs." In S. R. Komives and D. B. Woodard, Jr. (eds.), *Student Services: A Handbook for the Profession.* (4th ed.) San Francisco: Jossey-Bass, 2003.

Parham, T. A. *Psychological Storms: The African American Struggle for Identity.* Chicago: African American Images, 1993.

Rice, K. G. "Separation-Individuation and the Adjustment to College: A Longitudinal Study." *Journal of Counseling Psychology,* 1992, *39,* 203–213.

Richards, P. S. "Religious Devoutness in College Students: Relations with Emotional Adjustment and Psychological Separation from Parents." *Journal of Counseling Psychology,* 1991, *38,* 189-196.

Root, M.P.P. "A Bill of Rights for Racially Mixed People." In M.P.P. Root (ed.), *The Multiracial Experience: Racial Borders as the New Frontier.* Thousand Oaks, Calif.: Sage Publications, 1996.

Rotheram-Borus, M. J., and Fernandez, M. I. "Sexual Orientation and Developmental Challenges Experienced by Gay and Lesbian Youths." *Suicide and Life-Threatening Behavior,* 1995, *25 Supp.,* 26–34.

Samuolis, J., Layburn, K., and Schiaffino, K. M. "Identity Development and Attachment to Parents in College Students." *Journal of Youth and Adolescence,* 2001, *30,* 373–383.

Sanford, N. *The American College.* New York: Wiley, 1962.

Schlossberg, N. K., Waters, E. B., and Goodman, J. *Counseling Adults in Transition.* (2nd ed.) New York: Springer, 1995.

Schultheiss, D.E.P., and Blustein, D. L. "Contributions of Family Relationship Factors to the Identity Formation Process." *Journal of Counseling and Development,* 1994a, *73,* 159–166.

Schultheiss, D.E.P., and Blustein, D. L. "Role of Adolescent-Parent Relationships in College Student Development and Adjustment." *Journal of Counseling Psychology,* 1994b, *41,* 248–255.

Scott, B. R., and Daniel, B. V. "Why Parents of Undergraduates Matter to Higher Education." In B. V. Daniel and B. R. Scott (eds.), *Consumers, Adversaries, and Partners: Working with the Families of Undergraduates.* San Francisco: Jossey-Bass, 2001.

Shellenbarger, S. "Helicopter Parents Go to Work: Moms and Dads Are Now Hovering at the Office." *The Wall Street Journal,* March 16, 2006. Retrieved March 12, 2008, from http://online.wsj.com/article/SB114246499616999404.htm.

Sullivan, K., and Sullivan, A. "Adolescent-Parent Separation." *Developmental Psychology,* 1980, *16*(2), 93–99.

Tatum, B. D. *"Why Are All the Black Kids Sitting Together in the Cafeteria?" and Other Conversations About Race.* New York: Basic Books, 1997.

Taub, D. J. "Relationship of Selected Factors to Traditional-Age Undergraduate Women's Development of Autonomy." *Journal of College Student Development,* 1995, *36,* 141–151.

Taub, D. J. "Autonomy and Parental Attachment in Traditional-Age Undergraduate Women." *Journal of College Student Development,* 1997, *38,* 645–654.

Thornton, M. C. "Hidden Agendas, Identity Theories, and Multiracial People." In M.P.P. Root (ed.), *The Multiracial Experience: Racial Borders as the New Frontier.* Thousand Oaks, Calif.: Sage Publications, 1996.

Young, R. A., and Friesen, J. D. "The Intentions of Parents in Influencing the Career Development of Their Children." *The Career Development Quarterly,* 1992, *40,* 198–207.

DEBORAH J. TAUB is associate professor of higher education and coordinator of the Higher Education Program at The University of North Carolina at Greensboro.

NEW DIRECTIONS FOR STUDENT SERVICES • DOI: 10.1002/ss

3

As parents and other family members get more involved with their student's life, student affairs professionals must develop and deliver coherent, purposeful messages about the student experience.

Using Purposeful Messages to Educate and Reassure Parents

Jerry Price

In the cycle of a student's college life, student affairs professionals have opportunities to engage parents and families, including new student orientation, parent orientation, residence hall move-in days, and family weekends. On these occasions parents are searching for information about the institution and the experiences of their children. It is important that student affairs professionals be ready to provide this information and respond in a helpful and coherent manner.

However, many times there are important questions the parents don't ask—perhaps don't even know to ask. Student affairs professionals should anticipate these unasked questions and respond as if the parents are asking, "Please tell me what I really need to know about how to support my student." These interactions with parents—particularly the parents of new students—should be handled as open invitations to deliver the messages critical to student success.

To help prepare parents to be the most effective source of support for their students, student affairs professionals should deliver messages to parents that focus on the college environment, campus resources, the types of challenges their students may encounter, and how institutions and parents can work together to overcome these challenges. While much of this information may relate to issues and services outside the purview of student affairs, it is still appropriate for student affairs professionals to deliver these messages because they are typically the best prepared to help families understand the comprehensive nature of the student experience.

NEW DIRECTIONS FOR STUDENT SERVICES, no. 122, Summer 2008 © Wiley Periodicals, Inc.
Published online in Wiley InterScience (www.interscience.wiley.com) • DOI: 10.1002/ss.273

Understanding the Academic Environment and How It Works

Parents may lack a fundamental understanding of how a college or university is structured and functions. In the absence of better information, many parents will assume that institutions of higher education are similar to their student's high school or to the college the parents attended—inaccurate but certainly logical assumptions. Therefore, it is important that parents have a clear understanding of the structure and culture of higher education.

Academic Structure. At times the roles of deans, assistant and associate deans, department chairs, and especially faculty are unclear to those who work in higher education; it is not hard to imagine that many parents may not understand them at all. Nonetheless, these are the key players in the academic experience, so understanding these roles will help parents know whom their student should contact with academic concerns.

Faculty Relationship. The fundamental building block in the academic experience is the faculty member, so it makes sense to start there (Astin, 1993; Upcraft, Gardner, and Associates, 1989). Again, without better information, parents may assume that the role of the faculty member is comparable to that of a high school teacher. High school teachers went to college with the intent of being trained to teach. In contrast, many if not most college professors did not plan to be teachers; their dedication and commitment was not first to students, but to their discipline (and often still is). Parents often are surprised to learn that most college faculty have been trained almost exclusively in their individual disciplines and have had virtually no training in teaching.

Faculty Freedom and Autonomy. It also is critical that student affairs professionals introduce parents to the concept of academic freedom and the autonomous nature of the faculty. Although each academic department has a department chair, parents unfamiliar with higher education culture may construe the department chair as the faculty members' "boss." It is important to communicate that the faculty member is for the most part in an autonomous position: the faculty member independently develops the syllabus, designs the lectures and other class experiences, and determines the students' grades. A department chair cannot and will not step in to overturn a faculty member's decision.

It is the same for the role of the dean; the faculty are *led* by—not *supervised* by—a dean. True, there are policies and procedures for appealing faculty members' actions and decisions, and parents are well served to know about them; however, the existence of these policies does not negate the independent and autonomous role of the faculty member. Ultimately, the relationship between a student and a faculty member is key. Problems or misunderstandings are best resolved between the student and faculty member. The notion of "going over the faculty member's head" is misguided and rarely resolves a student's concern.

NEW DIRECTIONS FOR STUDENT SERVICES • DOI: 10.1002/ss

Academic Expectations: College Versus High School. Another important academic message for parents is the difference in academic expectations between high school and college. Parents logically can anticipate that college courses will be more difficult; however, they may not fully understand the nature of this difference. Despite the explosion of information technology around the world, colleges and universities are still fundamentally reading cultures. Students will be asked to read greater volumes of material and will be expected to comprehend the material fully. In the months leading up to the freshman year, parents would do well to encourage their students simply to read as much as they can to prepare for college coursework.

Another way in which the environment of colleges and universities differs from those in high school is the expected independence of the student. Unlike high school, most college classes will not have daily assignments designed to keep students on track; instead, college faculty will provide a syllabus that outlines the schedule for readings, papers, and exams throughout the semester. Students are expected to review the syllabus and use it as a tool to keep up on their own. Parents should encourage proper time management, since catching up in a college course is difficult.

Finally, a discussion on the nature of academic expectations in college provides a good opportunity to remind parents about the realities of the Federal Educational Right to Privacy Act (FERPA). In the K–12 system, FERPA states that the right to a student's record lies with the parent; parents not only have the right to see the student's record, they essentially are the owners of the record. That is why a parent legally can overrule the decision of her or his high school student, whether it is related to course selection or extracurricular activities (U.S. Department of Education, 2007).

Conversely, in college the rights to a student's record shift to the student, even if he or she is still a minor. Parents often push back when denied information about their children's academic performance, class attendance, discipline record, or other behavior. Student affairs professionals should help parents understand that it is best that this information now be provided to them by the student, not the institution.

Advising. Another critical step in a new student's path to starting college is selecting a major. Parents may not understand why their student's math ACT or SAT score might prohibit them from signing up for certain science courses, or why their daughter or son cannot double-major in music and accounting and still graduate in four years. They may perceive that prerequisites, accreditation requirements, and other academic factors are complicating the path their student may wish to take. The important message is that the institution has advisors who are knowledgeable about the factors involved in developing a course of study, and the student needs to work closely with them.

Understanding the Out-of-Class Environment

As confusing as the academic experience can be, parents may have just as many misconceptions about students' out-of-class opportunities and expectations. Just as parents may have assumed that a student's academic experience at college would be comparable to that in high school, likewise they may assume that students' out-of-class involvement at college would resemble their high school extracurricular activities.

Role of Student Development. To help parents understand why institutions do things the way they do, it might be helpful first to educate them on the concept of student development. Without this background, some of our policies and practices may seem illogical or ineffective. For example, to the parent of a new student who has had a conflict with a roommate, what sense does it make to require her or him to wait days or even weeks before making a roommate change? Why would an institution insist that a student organization's finances be handled by a student rather than its faculty advisor? Why would the residence life office let a student council set the quiet hours instead of the professional housing staff? When parents understand that the primary objective is not just eliminating mistakes but providing multiple opportunities for student learning, then they see these efforts differently.

Student Involvement. Student affairs professionals are well aware of the value of involvement in purposeful activities outside of the classroom because many studies have shown positive correlations between student involvement and retention rates, higher grades, and a variety of learning outcomes (Whitt and Miller, 1999; Astin, 1993). However, some parents may view these out-of-class opportunities as a respite from the pressure of classes; moreover, some parents may even see them as a diversion from their academic responsibilities. Indeed, for some students who commute from home, parents may become concerned when he or she has not returned home promptly after class. Parents may not recognize the value of their student remaining on campus for an organizational meeting, campus speaker, or leadership development workshop. Ironically, a student who spends more time with peers in such activities likely will have better grades and a higher retention rate (Study Group on the Conditions of Excellence in American Higher Education, 1984). Although this fact is well known to student affairs professionals, it could seem counterintuitive to those less familiar with college life.

Consequently, student affairs professionals would be advised not simply to communicate the value of out-of-class involvement to parents, but to lay out clearly the evidence in a convincing argument. Staff should persuade parents to become advocates for student involvement. Informed parents can become allies in the staff's efforts to promote students' purposeful involvement.

NEW DIRECTIONS FOR STUDENT SERVICES • DOI: 10.1002/ss

Residence Halls. Student affairs professionals know that residence halls are a key component of the out-of-class experience and contribute significantly to the quality of the student experience. Students who live on campus typically earn higher grades and have higher persistence rates (Blimling, 1989; Tinto, 1987). However, many parents have stereotypical perceptions of residence hall life and may have reservations about their student living on campus. Student affairs professionals must dispel these myths and stereotypes about residence halls and underscore their contribution to students' learning.

Not surprisingly, a major contributor to parents' skepticism about residence hall living is finances. For many, the cost of living on campus seems high compared to staying at home. For parents with this view, the message must start by helping them realize that the difference in cost is actually minimal. First, the cost of fuel for students driving back and forth to campus can be significant. The price of a residence hall contract usually includes meals, utilities, phone service, cable television, and Internet access. On many campuses, residence halls also contain a computer lab with around-the-clock availability. Although consideration of these items still may not make the cost of living on campus equivalent to living at home, it does provide a more accurate context for comparison.

Once parents understand the context of residence hall costs, the next step in the message is to underscore that the added value of the residence hall experience more than compensates for the difference in cost. One value to emphasize is the time saved from commuting to campus; for the student whose home is half an hour's drive from campus, he or she can invest the hour commute in reading, studying, research in the library, or talking with a professor. A second value to emphasize is the benefit of a new student's interactions with peers: the more connected a new student feels to her or his fellow students, the more connected the student will feel to the school (Astin, 1993). Fortunately, the benefit of their child making meaningful friendships is a value parents understand and have long embraced.

The Role of Institutional Culture.   Not all student affairs programs and professionals approach their work in the same way. Institutions develop their own set of policies and procedures within the context of student development. However, to gain a more complete picture, parents also need to know about an institution's unique culture.

Parents are particularly interested in institutional policies about their being informed of students' progress. Does the institution permit a parent to sit in with the student during orientation advising? Are there mechanisms for sending the student's grades to the parents? Are parents alerted if the student is in danger of being suspended? There are different ways of dealing with these and other situations, and it is important for parents to understand how the institution's specific policies apply. Once again, this may be

NEW DIRECTIONS FOR STUDENT SERVICES • DOI: 10.1002/ss

another opportunity to remind parents about FERPA and the limitations on sharing information with parents.

Understanding and Accessing Campus Resources

Another message to parents that can have a significant impact on their students' success is the availability of campus resources. Parents should know what resources are available to students to support their academic and personal success. Parents need to know not only for their own peace of mind, but also in order to remind their students of these resources' availability and potential value. Although these resources are usually shared with students during orientation and welcome week activities, many traditional-age students are so focused on making friends and exploring new social opportunities that they may not retain much of the information. However, parents often pay careful attention to these matters and can be effective referral agents for their children.

Resources for Students.   There is a long list of services and resources that institutions may offer to students. Following is a list of the campus resources that may be of particular interest to parents.

Tutoring.   Parents will want to know what types of resources are available to help a student succeed academically. Staff should educate them on any tutoring services the institution provides and whether these services are covered by a student service fee already paid by the students or whether a separate fee will apply.

Library.   Research papers can be among the most intimidating tasks for a new student, and the expectations for such papers vary widely across high schools. Parents may want to learn about research resources in the campus library and to what extent staff are available for students who need help getting started.

Advising.   As mentioned earlier, selecting a major and the appropriate courses can be stressful for students. Parents will want to understand how a student receives help with the selection of classes for the coming term. They also may want to know where the student can go if he or she feels the advisor's instructions are unclear or inaccurate. Parents can become particularly uneasy if their child changes their major during or after the first year and will want help understanding how the student can identify a new course of study and still stay on schedule.

Student employment.   Many students will need to work while in school to help pay the bills or cover personal expenses. Others may want to work simply for the experience or the extra spending money. For example, because several studies indicate that students who work on campus often earn higher grades (Astin, 1984), student affairs professionals would serve parents well by promoting on-campus employment. They can inform parents of job opportunities available to students on campus and how students can apply for them.

Health services. Parents are just as concerned about their student's personal health and well-being as they are about their academic progress. This is particularly true if the student is living on campus. Parents will have great interest in the services available to the student who gets ill. Staff should explain the scope of their health services—including emergency services—and their hours of availability; if services are available only during business hours, parents should be informed of where students should go on evenings or weekends. Also, each year new students come to campus with existing medical conditions that need ongoing attention; for these parents, the quality of health care available on campus is a major consideration. If parents can meet the health services staff and discuss the student's medical needs, they will feel much more at ease. Depending on the student's medical condition, it also may be beneficial to make connections with medical specialists in the community.

Counseling services. Parents may likewise be concerned about their student's emotional health and how well they are adjusting to college life. How are their students handling the stresses of college academics and their new environment? Perhaps the student is already emotionally vulnerable when he or she arrives on campus due to a loss in the family or a recently ended relationship. Whatever the issue, parents will want to know that trained professionals are available to provide support. As with physical health issues, many students arrive on campus each year needing treatment for depression or other psychological conditions. In addition to coordinating with health services regarding any medication needs, parents may want to consult with counseling staff on therapy options. In some cases, these therapy options may include off-campus resources.

Campus ministries. For many students, opportunities to continue their spiritual growth and nourishment while at college are very important; not surprisingly, this is a priority for many parents as well. These parents will appreciate any information on the various religious communities on- and off-campus. They also may want insights into the spiritual life on campus to ascertain to what extent it is consistent with those of the family.

Dean of students office. While parents usually appreciate receiving information on all of these services and resources, they may also feel a little overwhelmed by it all. For this reason, another important piece of information to communicate to parents is a contact of last resort—a person or office available to their student in the event he or she does not know where else to go. On many campuses this is the dean of students office. Regardless of who it is, parents will want to know where to direct a student who seems unsure of where to turn.

Student Resources and Parental Boundaries. By educating parents on these resources, student affairs professionals are providing parents with tools to help their son or daughter. By being aware of these resources, parents can encourage their students to seek out the appropriate help; however, parents must understand that once students pursue these services, the interaction will be between the institution and the student. Unless the student requests her or his parents be involved and signs a waiver to that effect, parental involvement typically will be limited.

In some cases, parents are not intruding into the student's business—their involvement has been requested by the student. For example, since making decisions about majors and long-term academic goals can be very stressful, students often will seek counsel from their parents and may want their parents present during appointments. However, institutions must make clear to both parents and students that these decisions belong to the student and that the parents' involvement—even when solicited by the student—will be considered strictly advisory by the institution.

While the student-parent-institution relationship is driven primarily by privacy policies, student affairs professionals also need to help parents understand the developmental reasons for this practice. In their work with students, student affairs professionals are not only helping students address the immediate concern, but are also trying to teach them problem-solving and coping skills. To accomplish this aim, it usually is best if parents play a supporting rather than active role in the process.

Parent Resources. In addition to information about resources available to students, institutions should make sure their messages to parents also include any resources available to parents. Many campuses have a parent association that serves as a resource for parents as well as an opportunity to get involved in their child's institution; likewise, some campuses have an office of parent programs with a staff specifically trained to work with parents. Even if neither of these options exist, more and more campuses have developed a web site specifically for parents; such web sites contain much of the information discussed above.

Finally, many parents appreciate having a primary contact or point-of-entry of their own as well. Most parents recognize that when students enroll in college they are now responsible for managing their own academic career and solving their own challenges. However, even parents who have embraced this concept still feel more at ease knowing whom they could call if their child needed someone's intervention. Whether it is the dean of students office, parent office, or some other campus resource, this contact should be a part of the message communicated to parents.

Understanding the Typical Challenges Students Encounter

In developing the desired messages to deliver to parents, remember that parents are looking to us not only for information but also for a sense of comfort. They want reassurance—as much as reasonably can be offered—that their son or daughter will avoid major problems and have a successful college experience. They also want to know how the institution will respond if the student does encounter serious problems, and whether and how the parents will be informed. Therefore, our message to parents must include a candid discussion of these issues as well.

It is not uncommon for students to experience struggles during their college experience. While parents may recognize this, they may not understand the specific challenges students face, and they may not feel confident distinguishing routine struggles from serious ones. Student affairs professionals can assist parents by preparing them for the typical challenges students encounter during college and educating them on how to help the students work through these challenges.

Academic transition. For many students, the biggest challenge will be college-level academics. Even students with strong high school academic records may experience disappointing grades on early exams or papers; in fact, for some students, college may be the first time the student experiences a grade below an A or B. In these situations, the student can become very discouraged—and parents are likely to pick up on it. Often the student is just caught off guard by the large volume of reading and assignments, while in other cases the student is simply adjusting to the higher grading expectations of college. If either of these is the case, student affairs professionals can comfort parents by assuring them that these are typical academic adjustments experienced by many students. Not only are they common, but most students experiencing these kinds of problems bounce back quickly.

Loss of academic focus. In some cases, a particularly poor academic showing during the first semester could be a symptom of a student's lost focus or motivation. As the parents discuss the problem with their student, they should first try to ascertain whether the student is going to class regularly or is socializing with friends regularly instead. If either of these is the case, it could be the sign of a problem with long-term academic consequences if not addressed early. Furthermore, if the student has fallen into an alcohol or drug abuse situation, there can be health and legal consequences as well. Student affairs professionals should not try to tell parents how to parent, but they can educate parents on what they know about various student behaviors and their impact on student success.

Homesickness. For students attending college away from home, one challenge may be homesickness. Hearing their child experience loneliness can leave parents feeling particularly helpless and heartbroken. The message in this situation is to suggest that parents be positive and encouraging in their interactions with their students. If the parents panic, the student may panic as well. The key to overcoming homesickness is to develop a new support network on campus. Parents should encourage students to get involved, perhaps by joining a student organization, intramural sports team, or other activity through which they can meet students with similar interests. The parent also should reinforce that meeting new friends often means taking some personal risks.

More serious concerns. Unfortunately, some college students do find themselves in more serious situations. Inform parents of how the institution intends to respond should a serious situation occur, such as a medical emergency, a mental health emergency, or an alcohol or drug abuse problem. Parents want to know how the student's academics will be affected by the emergency or an extended absence from classes. They will feel more comfortable if they believe the institution is prepared to respond effectively in the event of an emergency.

Parental involvement. Of course, parents will be particularly interested in the institution's procedures and policies when contacting parents. Even if the institution cannot guarantee that parents will be contacted in all situations, it is still beneficial for the institution and the parents to reconcile expectations regarding parental contact.

Tailoring Messages for Different Populations of Parents

While all parents can benefit from learning more about the institution and the student experience, the information that parents want and need is driven very much by their background. Student affairs professionals need to be sensitive to these various backgrounds and consider seriously how best to shape their message.

Parents of First-Generation Students. Many parents are college graduates themselves, and although college life likely has changed considerably since their days on campus, they nonetheless know the fundamentals of the college experience. Some parents may not have attended college themselves but have sent previous children to college; these parents also understand the basics of the college experience. However, parents of first-generation students are usually unfamiliar with—and often intimidated by—the college environment. These parents will benefit from some strong foundational information for context before they can make sense of the issues more readily understood by parents with college experience.

One example of this issue is the financial processes of higher education. An institution should educate parents about its specific financial policies and procedures, but for the parents of first-generation students the entire process can still seem like a mystery. Why are there different types of tuition, and what is the difference between tuition and fees? Why do I pay some fees and not others? How does my child's financial aid get on my bill? These and similar questions can be overwhelming to parents, and it is important for student affairs professionals to provide a basic foundation of the overall process first before reviewing more specific institutional issues.

On-campus housing is another area in which the parents of first-generation students can often benefit from such foundational information. Parents who lived on campus while in college usually do not need an explanation of the value of the on-campus experience—they experienced it themselves. However, for the families of first-generation parents, living on campus may be seen merely as a convenience because they live too far for the student to commute. For students who live within driving distance of campus, then, the option of living on campus may not even be considered by the parents because the value of living at home seems so logical. From their perspective, they may see living at home as providing some stability in the student's otherwise tense transition to college; they also may believe the home environment is more conducive to good study habits than a building with hundreds of other young adults living in it. The fact that living with a large group of strangers is better for a new student than living at home may seem counterintuitive. Student affairs professionals' ability to make the case for the value of on-campus housing can potentially make the difference between a student who will benefit from living on campus and one who commutes from home.

Parents of African American Students. On top of the more universal parental concerns, the parents of African American students—particularly those at predominantly White institutions—often have additional issues and anxieties. Issues of students' personal health and safety may take on a different dimension for these parents. The nature of the neighboring environment and the availability of community resources may be more significant for them. In communicating with parents of African American students, it is particularly important for student affairs professionals to establish a sense of trust—to reassure parents that staff members are sensitive to the unique challenges of African American students and will work just as diligently for their success (Freeman, 2007).

Parents of Hispanic Students. Because many Hispanic students are often the first generation to attend college, their parents will encounter challenges similar to those of African American parents, and these parents must often contend with language and cultural complications as well. Parents with undeveloped English skills may feel isolated from and unwelcome by the institution; even those parents who speak some English may not have the vocabulary needed to understand conversations about higher education. By making important information for parents available in Spanish as well as English, institutions can help bridge this gap. However, understanding cultural differences can be just as important as addressing language barriers. For example, in many Hispanic families specific expectations accompany the roles of parent and child; furthermore, these expectations may have significant differences depending on gender (Mena and Guardia, 2007). It is important that student affairs professionals show respect for these cultural values as they educate parents on the services, policies, and procedures of the institution.

Parents of International Students. Family dynamics can also be an issue when working with the parents of international students. International students often come from cultures in which parents have the right to receive their students' academic records, disciplinary files, and even their residence hall guest registry. To these parents, explanations of FERPA or other American laws and policies often just make the staff appear uncooperative. Again, these parents are entitled to a patient, respectful conversation about how American higher education institutions work. Another complicating factor for many international students is their financing. Many international students come from families with financial hardship, yet they are not eligible for most of the financial aid programs available to U.S. citizens; in many cases, international students' families have sacrificed much of their finances just to get their child to the United States and enrolled in college. Student affairs professionals must ensure these parents understand the financial reality of their student's situation.

Essential Message: Partners Aiming for the Same Goal

As institutions and parents communicate about the student's experience at college, it can be easy to get caught up in small details or debates over specific institutional policies or procedures. If student affairs professionals allow themselves to get too involved in these debates, parents may completely miss the larger message: institutions and parents are partners aiming for the same goal—the success of their son or daughter. True, there may be times the student finds herself or himself in trouble, and, yes, it is very possible that in some situations student affairs professionals may not be able to contact the parents about it. Nonetheless, parents must believe that the student is in good hands and the institution is well prepared to assist their child in many ways. It is the job of both parent and institution to support the student and encourage her or him to succeed—the parties just perform this job in different ways. If student affairs professionals are successful in communicating this message, all other messages become much easier.

References

Astin, A. W. "Student Involvement: A Development Theory for Higher Education." *Journal of College Student Development,* 1984, *25,* 297–308.

Astin, A. W. *What Matters in College?* San Francisco: Jossey-Bass, 1993.

Blimling, G. S. "A Meta-Analysis of the Influence of College Residence Halls on Academic Performance." *Journal of College Student Development,* 1989, *30,* 298–308.

Freeman, M. A. "Working with Parents of African American Students." *Leadership Exchange,* 2007, 5(1), 17.

Kuh, G. D., Schuh, J. H., Whitt, E. J., and Associates. *Involving Colleges.* San Francisco: Jossey-Bass, 1991.

Mena, S. B., and Guardia, J. R. "No Parent Left Behind: A Primer on Understanding Latino Parents." *Leadership Exchange,* 2007, (5)1, 19.

Study Group on the Conditions of Excellence in American Higher Education. *Involvement in Learning*. Washington, D.C.: U.S. Department of Education, 1984.

Tinto, V. *Leaving College: Rethinking the Causes and Cures of Student Attrition*. Chicago: University of Chicago Press, 1987.

Upcraft, M. L., Gardner, J. N., and Associates. *The Freshman Year Experience: Helping Students Survive and Succeed in College*. San Francisco: Jossey-Bass, 1989.

U.S. Department of Education. "Family Educational Rights and Privacy Act." 2007. Retrieved Jan. 22, 2007, from www.ed.gov/policy/gen/guid/fpco/ferpa/index.html.

Whitt, E. J., and Miller, T. E. "Student Learning Outside the Classroom: What Does the Research Tell Us?" In E. J. Whitt (ed.), *Student Learning as Student Affairs Work: Responding to Our Imperative*. NASPA Monograph Series, 1999, *23*, 51–62.

Jerry Price is associate vice president and dean of students at The University of Texas–Pan American.

4

Interaction with parents and family members continues to increase on college campuses across the nation. This chapter reviews best practices for communicating with and programming for parents and family members of enrolled students.

Capitalizing on Parent and Family Partnerships Through Programming

Jeanine A. Ward-Roof, Patrick M. Heaton, Mary B. Coburn

Since the 1980s, parent and family member programming efforts have varied widely across the nation. To best prepare campus for the onset of parent and family involvement, the authors suggest the following strategies:

1. Assess parent and family needs
2. Set program goals
3. Secure resources
4. Staff appropriately
5. Create consistent messages that set limits and offer opportunities for appropriate involvement
6. Communicate often
7. Include parents and family members in crisis planning and programming
8. Educate students on how to develop appropriate relationships with their parents

We believe these eight strategies are paramount when developing parent and family member programming and outreach.

Before the 1980s, parents were not identified as an influential campus population. Cohen (1985) states although parents were not a huge entity on campus, he found some individual parents did engage professionals looking for specific information and advice via phone, letter, or campus visit. However, twenty years later, the trend has changed greatly. Pennington observes: "The late twentieth and early twenty-first centuries have brought

NEW DIRECTIONS FOR STUDENT SERVICES, no. 122, Summer 2008 © Wiley Periodicals, Inc.
Published online in Wiley InterScience (www.interscience.wiley.com) • DOI: 10.1002/ss.274

with them a new sense of parenting and a need for higher education professionals to reevaluate and readjust the ways in which they work and relate to students. Through partnerships with parents . . . , we can create additional learning opportunities and also increase the likelihood of student success" (2005, p. ix). Moreover, evolving editions of *Letting Go: A Parents' Guide to Understanding College Years* (Coburn and Treeger, 1988, 2003) also demonstrate how information for parents has changed over the decades. The initial edition of their book was one of the first publications for parents designed to help develop a better understanding of the issues their students and they would encounter throughout the college experience. These issues included letting go, getting involved, understanding college stress, and a general introduction to the campus culture. The later edition discussed many of the same issues and covered additional complex problems that students and their families must address such as relationships, alcohol and drug use, and date rape. The literature clearly displays the changes parents and family members have initiated over the past two decades. Parents and family are now beginning to better understand how those changes affect the practice of higher education. Because of these changes in higher education practice, staff and administrators continue to find programming and outreach for parents a necessity and an asset. Furthermore, new parental behaviors—often described as helicopter-like because of their hovering about campus—and newly defined family structures also illustrate this reality. The free-spirited students of the 1960s are now the helicopter parents of millennial students. To further illustrate these changes, Merriman's (2006) survey of student affairs professionals found parent interactions have increased at a rate of 93 percent over the past five years. All of these combined variables drastically change the ways parents desire to be included in the educational process.

To accommodate and embrace the increase in parental involvement, programming and outreach have become positive means to connect with parents early in a student's college experience, though some administrators argue that many parents are so fully engaged that their involvement suspends or retards the development of their children. Woollen (2005) concurs by citing how some parents of today's college students have surpassed appropriate involvement levels and can be defined as intrusive. They defined such intrusive behaviors as parents editing college papers, complaining to faculty about course or assignment grades, contacting academic advisors about class times, and attending career fairs with their students. Additionally, the introduction and proliferation of cell phones, e-mail, instant messaging, and the like perpetuate these acts, causing administrators to view students and parents or family members as seemingly attached via their technological umbilical cord. Thus, during a medical visit it is not unusual for a student to hand his or her cell phone to a health center doctor saying, "My mother wants to discuss this with you." Technology connects parents and family members to campus in ways never experienced before, and often parents and family members are apprised of their son's or daughter's situation on campus before staff and administrators. At times, these interactions make it difficult for staff to appropriately respond to situations or to the student(s) involved without emotional external influences.

Mullendore, Banahan, and Ramsey (2005) predicted that student affairs professionals would be most effective if they could be proactive when working with the new models, assumptions, and expectations of parents and family members. Merriman (2006, p. 48) noted, "Parents and parent expectations are redefining the work of student affairs professionals as they expect institutions to respond to all of their concerns, protect their students, and expeditiously resolve any crisis they encounter." In response to these new parent expectations, staff and administrators across the nation continue to develop more and more opportunities for parent and family involvement. This chapter will describe some of the programming and outreach efforts common on college and university campuses, such as orientation, parent-family weekend, little siblings' weekends and events, opening convocation and graduation ceremonies, electronic outreach and communication, and parent associations.

Orientation

Including parents and family members in campus orientation programs is paramount. Jacobs and With (2002) concur, observing that parents who are included in the orientation process view their involvement as an illustration of their partnership in the education of their child. Furthermore, Mullendore and Banahan (2005) suggest that campus administrators should begin outreach to parents and families early, in order to channel their energies into positive interactions. Moreover, Hatch (2003) believes parental support has been known to influence student success, and Turrentine, Schnure, Ostroth, and Ward-Roof (2000) assert that student expectations can be influenced by parental beliefs. Orientation programs are clear opportunities to include, engage, and partner with parents and family members in their students' educational process and assist the student, parent, family members, and campus staff in establishing expectations for involvement.

Jacobs and With (2002) observe that parents must be provided with valuable campus information so they can assist their students generally. Furthermore, the most recently published National Orientation Directors Association Databank (Strumpf, 2000) revealed that 100 percent of the institutions who responded offered some type of parent orientation program in conjunction with or separately from student orientation. Although the delivery and timing of the program varied by institution, the responses suggest that including parents and families in the orientation process has been a common practice for many years.

When implementing parent orientation programs, Austin (2003) found that two specific considerations need to be addressed: content and structure. Ward-Roof (2005) suggests implementing the following steps when developing an orientation program. First, staff must assess the parent-family population to determine their needs. Characteristics such as number of first-generation, legacy, ethnic diversity, and single-parent status can affect the program offerings. Second, decisions need to be made about the duration of the programming offered. Parents of traditional eighteen- to twenty-year-old students often will attend one- to two-day orientation programs with their students, whereas family members of nontraditional students may be more likely to attend a weekend or evening program. Other models include online resources, a series of meetings, week-long events, written information, or shorter time frames of interactions. The third step is determining when the program will be offered and what content should be included. Timing for orientation programs is typically preterm, summer, fall, spring, or a hybrid of these types. Campus resources and parent-family needs and will also need to be considered when setting suitable times for parent-family members' orientation programs.

Austin (2003) suggests that staff members working in the orientation program should convey knowledge about and genuine interest in parent-family involvement. Furthermore, the following topics should be addressed during the programming: handling crisis, decreasing levels of parental control, challenges of renegotiating roles, ways for parents to deal with their own life changes, understanding of academic year and stresses, time management, redefining participation in each other's lives, vehicles to discuss changes and parent-family reactions, campus tours, policy and procedure, programs, student life concerns, financial issues, opportunities to meet campus community, information about first-year (and subsequent year) programming, and information about campus environment and surrounding areas. Other specific topics we suggest including are a better understanding of the Family Education Rights and Privilege Act (FERPA) and other specific laws and policies of the state and institution; expectations for appropriate involvement; and opportunities to meet and interact with current students, parents and family members of current students, and community members. In addition, we recommend discussing when members of the institution will contact parents and family members (such as alcohol violations, suicide attempts, or other grave situations) and what parents and family members can do if they are concerned about their children.

Mental health issues should also be a topic for consideration within orientation programming. Educating parents and family members about mental health issues, resources, and realities is a necessity. Often, parents and family members of incoming students believe a change in environment will erase current mental health issues. Orientation is an optimal time for encouraging parents and family members to have conversations about medication, counseling, and other mental health needs in order to help their sons or daughters be successful.

Other options for orientation programs include parent-family hand-books or calendars. These can be designed to remind parents about the messages and expectations the campus community has for their involvement. Furthermore, the publications can assist parents with a better understanding of campus policy and practice, as well as expectations for the students during the year. Parent-family handbooks or calendars are also a way to empower parents and families to encourage their students' learning about and use of campus resources. Current examples are publications that outline specific situations and contacts where parents and family members should send their students. For instance, instead of calling the president's office about a roommate situation, the publication might offer tips for parents as their children resolve issues, including phone numbers, e-mail addresses, and other contact information for housing staff members who are more skilled at addressing these specific issues.

Web sites are another positive way to program for parents before and after orientation programs. Little information is static in today's technological world. Using web sites that link parents and family members to campus resources enables staff to offer them the latest information. In times of crisis, web sites are also excellent vehicles for quickly informing parents and family members about campus news and safety tips.

Survey Results

Much of the programming being offered to parents and other family members is guided by institutional resources, philosophy toward parent engagement, and desired outcomes. Wanting to better understand the breadth and depth of programming being offered on today's campuses, we surveyed institutions about best practices and challenges in this area. An invitation to complete a thirteen-question online survey was distributed by e-mail to college and university administrators belonging to American College and University Housing Officers International (ACUHO-I) and National Orientation Directors Association (NODA). This invitation yielded 101 responses, 88 of which were from nonduplicate institutions. Controlling for institutions with multiple respondents, 74.26 percent of the participants were from public institutions and 25.74 percent from private institutions. When asked to identify their institution as being primarily residential or commuter, representation was 66.34 percent and 38.61 percent, respectively.

When asked to identify audiences targeted through parent-family programming, 95.56 percent of respondents named parents, 47.78 percent named guardians, and 34.44 percent named extended family. Less often mentioned were grandparents (21.11 percent), spouses (21.11 percent), siblings (20 percent), and partners (18.89 percent). The least targeted audiences were children (11 percent) and friends (10 percent) of students. When respondents were asked to name the topics covered in parent-family

New Directions for Student Services • DOI: 10.1002/ss

orientation programs, most commonly identified were safety (85.06 percent), housing (81.61 percent), opportunities to interact with administrators (78.16 percent), financial aid (78.16 percent), health and counseling services (77.01 percent), student involvement (77.01 percent), social adjustment (75.86 percent), family role in student transition (74.71 percent), Federal Education Right to Privacy Act (FERPA) (73.56 percent), academic expectations (72.41 percent), and food service (71.26 percent). In contrast, the topics least commonly covered included opportunities to interact with alumni (17.24 percent), nonacademic honor policies (14.94 percent), information about the local community (26.44 percent), interactions with parents of current students (28.74 percent), academic honor codes (29.89 percent), and opportunities to interact with faculty (51.72 percent). When asked which services and programs were offered beyond orientation, respondents most commonly mentioned parent-family web sites (65.88 percent), parent-family weekends (60 percent), electronic newsletters (57.65 percent), handbooks (44.71 percent), associations or advisory boards (42.35 percent), and calendars (37.65 percent). Least frequently mentioned were professional and social networking (15.29 percent), e-mail listservs (18.8 percent), and printed newsletters (28.24 percent).

Respondents were also asked to identify institutional best practices in programming for parents and family members. As the answers to that question were analyzed, three significant themes emerged. Frequently cited as important was the shift toward viewing parents as stakeholders in the student experience. One respondent wrote, "The philosophy behind our parent/family program is that we view them as partners, not helicopter parents or people who need to let go. We have found that by empowering parents/families with resources we all can spend our time together focusing on student success, instead of telling parents/families what they cannot do." The idea of institutional collaboration was also frequently mentioned. Viewing parent programming as a shared responsibility that requires buy-in from multiple academic and student affairs units was noted to be a successful technique for diffusing costs, increasing programming contacts, and addressing the holistic developmental needs of students. The final best practice to emerge as a theme in survey responses was the use of electronic publications and web sites as cost-efficient and flexible ways to communicate with parents and extended family members.

In addition to best practices, respondents always mentioned several challenges they have faced in parent programming. The most significant of these challenges seems to be the lack of funding and staff support: the absence of an appropriate level of resources, money, or staffing was mentioned by 74 percent of respondents. Other challenges included addressing the widely diverse needs of parents, disconnect between institutional strategic priorities and the philosophy behind parent programming, and geographic distance between the institution and some students' families.

Electronic Outreach and Communication

As evident in the survey, technology can be an effective way to reach parents and family members, because most are now somewhat familiar with navigating web pages, downloading newsletters, or registering for a listserv. Often during these interactions administrators will hear parents and family members refer to a web page, stating they were not able to find the information online, or the web page and newsletter offered conflicting information. As parents and family members become technologically savvy, more information has been moved to formats accessible through the Internet, such as electronic newsletters, informative and question-oriented listservs, webcams showing the campus or a particular event on campus, online parent-family surveys, registration information for parent-family events, and e-mail communications. Although technology is an effective way to release volumes of information to parents and family members and is accessible twenty-four hours a day, those who use the technology often demand answers and feedback more quickly. To illustrate this concept, Merriman's (2006) research identifies technology as a reason for increased parental involvement, now that parents have continuous access to information and contact with their students. Consistent with this research, we have received e-mail communications from a parent or family member at 2:00 a.m. demanding resolution to a situation by 8:00 a.m.

In spite of these drawbacks, providing information electronically to parents and family members can be a cost-saving measure. The new challenge for staff and administrators is maintaining the content and quickly answering the questions of parents and family members who use the Internet to communicate and obtain up-to-date information.

Parent-Family Weekends

Parent-family weekends provide an excellent opportunity for parents and family members to visit and engage with their students' college environment; however, the timing of these weekends is important. The delicate balance allows students (especially new students) enough time to adjust to their campus environment and also gives parents and family members enough time to adjust to their home environment without their son or daughter.

In addition, providing a fulfilling program can only benefit the campus and the parents' and families' relationships. Programs for a parent-family weekend can be scheduled for one weekend, a series of weekends, or through a variety of different events. Models include programming around a large event such as a sporting event or campus tradition, offering a series of weekends during fall and spring terms, or labeling a series of artistic or campus events as a parent-family weekend. Assessing the needs and desires of parents in light of campus resources is the best way to discover which model would be most appropriate for an institution. Many campus staff have trouble deciding how centralized parent-family weekends should be—they want to include all aspects of campus, but don't want to sponsor traditional organization events. One example of this challenge is to include individual registered student organization programming during the formal schedule along with campus office and departmental programming even though staff members have little knowledge about the activities offered. Those involved with planning the weekends are charged with weighing the centralization of weekend events and the inclusion of the campus with the outcomes of the programming offered to best decide what should be included.

Fees are another consideration for parent-family weekends. Many institutions find it necessary to charge participants for meals, tours, and space, whereas others gather the resources within the established budget to cover the costs associated with the events.

Nonetheless, parent-family weekends are opportunities for campus staff and administration to showcase student achievement, research, entertainment, resources, campus awards, and unique campus traditions. In addition, parents and family members should have opportunities to interact with faculty and staff, tour campus facilities, and meet those who are important to their son or daughter. These interactions are good times to emphasize the messages outlined in orientation and help parents and family members continue to develop positive relationships with staff, faculty, and administrators.

Younger Siblings Events

Programming for siblings can be a stand-alone event or intertwined with other offerings such as orientation or parent-family weekend. Regardless of the type of program format, similarities exist among offerings. Typical activities included in a younger siblings event might be interactions with the institution mascot, book clubs, recreation time, motivational speakers on setting goals for college attendance, sporting events, tours, visits to classrooms, and taking advantage of the unique features of an institution. Ultimately, programming for siblings is a great way to positively influence family commitment to an institution specifically for the student in attendance and in the future for the sibling at the programming.

Opening Convocation and Graduation

Traditional ceremonies are excellent opportunities for parents and family members to get involved in their students' campus lives. Many institutions offer opening convocations as a way for parents and family members to acknowledge the separation of the family unit. The inspiration and building of a class are a means by which members of the community gather together to celebrate the beginning of a new phase of life, often with their parents and family members supporting them through the process. Convocations typically include a welcome to the community; an explanation of

NEW DIRECTIONS FOR STUDENT SERVICES • DOI: 10.1002/ss

culture and rituals; a celebration of the beginning of college; an opportunity to meet faculty, staff, and peer students; and motivational words to inspire achievement.

Graduation ceremonies are phenomenal ways for parents and family members to celebrate the accomplishments of their students with the campus community. These typically traditional ceremonies signify the end of college and the beginning of the students' transition into their next phase of life. Similar to the opening convocation, these ceremonies recognize the parents and family members as a significant source of support and include a celebration of the accomplishments of the graduates.

Parent Associations

In our survey 42.35 percent of respondents reported that parent associations were used to channeling parent and family member energy to best serve the campus community. Merriman's (2006) broader survey found 60 percent of those campuses surveyed currently supported a parent association. With the proliferation of technology, communicating with the parent association and individual parents and family members has become easier, but also more demanding. Many parent associations have developed electronic listservs, newsletters, or combinations of the two to keep parents and family members informed of recent events and policy changes, celebrate milestones, or distribute invitations to events. Parent associations can foster the development of ambassadors for the institution across the nation, and the use of these ambassadors to inform others about challenges, celebrations, and opportunities create positive outcomes for the institution and the association. Other institutional benefits to hosting a parent association are the development of a strong connection between parents and family members and the institution, opportunities to explain how changes will affect the lives of the students, and the development of a pool of volunteers who are committed to the institutional mission and goals. Benefits of membership for the parents and family members include discounts on services within the community, opportunities to stay involved in their son's or daughter's life, learning more about campus programs and activities, increased contact with campus resources, and becoming part of an established network of parents who can answer questions and offer support.

There is no clear reporting structure for parent associations, but the two most popular reporting lines are within student affairs or the fundraising or alumni division. Regardless of the reporting line, developing parent associations staff must establish a clear purpose for the creation of the association and, with the group members, establish a constitution, bylaws, or both to support the mission of the institution, expectations for involvement, and descriptions of functions, roles, reporting lines, and responsibilities. It is also advisable to create an orientation for new board members to help them best understand their roles, responsibilities, and limitations. In cases where these steps are underdeveloped, rogue associations that contradict the goals and needs of the institutions can develop. Common purposes for parent associations are to serve as ambassadors for the institution, to assist with the realization of the mission, to fundraise or identify prospective people or companies for development activities, to advocate for issues or concerns with state representatives or within the institution structure, or to support the success of students. Parents or family members who are approached about joining an association often liken it to membership in a high school booster club or PTA, but parent associations aim at different goals, such as helping students succeed, helping institutions realize their mission, and helping parents adjust to their new roles without participating directly in their sons' and daughters' activities.

Parent associations often develop into fundraising entities or parent offices or services on campuses. If one or both of these paths are taken or desired at an institution, be sure that staff involved are knowledgeable about current student and parent and family member issues and needs. In addition, train staff to be able to diffuse situations and help parents and family members remember and maintain their roles on campus. If fundraising becomes a specific role of the association, the purpose of the fundraising should also be clearly delineated at the onset, ensuring the dollars raised meet the desired needs of the campus and the association combined. Fundraising dollars can be channeled to meet specific programming or event needs such as purchasing software, improving campus lighting, hiring special staff, supporting upcoming events, or offering professional development. And if the fundraising role of the parent-family association is fully realized, the sponsoring division can establish the exclusive right to target parents and family members in their development efforts.

Along with fundraising, additional roles parent association members adopt might include helping recruit new students by writing letters; attending college fairs; answering questions or directing potential students to campus resources; hosting receptions for incoming students before enrollment to connect those from the same geographical area; supporting parents and family members; offering expert guidance on campus move-in, selection of vendors, budgeting, and getting involved; serving as a parent or family member voice to the campus community by voicing their thoughts on policy and procedure change, serving on search committees or review or advisory boards; and creating and presenting awards to the campus community.

Some of the numerous models for parent associations include those who offer membership to any parent or family member with a currently enrolled student, those who cultivate fee-based memberships during orientation or other pre-enrollment activities, and hybrid versions of each. The choice of these models should be based on the campus resources available and the needs of the parent and family members.

Regardless of the type of parent-family programming being developed, the common denominator is to establish a set of agreed-upon messages for parents and family members and consistently emphasize those messages throughout the programming and outreach. Ultimately, we believe that parents, staff, and administrators hold the same goals for the students: to mature and be empowered to become a positive force in a global society. It is our opinion that engaging programming opportunities for and effective outreach to parents and family members enables the development and emphasis of appropriate involvement for parents.

Hurt and others (2003) studied how student affairs administrators spent their time. They discovered that 23 percent of their time was spent communicating, and this included communication with family members of both current and prospective students. In light of that finding, the following are suggestions for programming to parents and family members.

1. *Assess parent and family needs.* First and foremost, take the time to find out who the parents and family members are and what they need. Assessing the population will enable the staff to best design programming for the unique population at your institution. Assessment can take place during current programming, more formally through surveys developed and implemented by institutional research staff, or qualitatively when discussing issues with parents and family members. Assessment is discussed in greater detail in Chapter Six.

2. *Set program and outreach goals.* Regardless of the type of programming or outreach offered, goals should be established and revisited often. In addition, these goals should align with the mission of the institution and be widely accepted by parents and family members.

3. *Secure resources.* Strong programming and outreach need appropriate resources. Assess what is needed and find means to secure the needed resources through fees, campus resources, or outside sponsorship.

4. *Staff appropriately.* Parents and family members need a tremendous amount of support and guidance. Be sure that staffing exists and is responsive to the needs of the parents and family members. Adequate staffing can assist the parents and family members in channeling their energies and emotions appropriately when issues arise.

5. *Communicate often.* Staff cannot overcommunicate with parents and family members. Develop the best means for communicating with families—whether electronically or through newsletters or mailings—and use them for all messages.

6. *Use programming to educate students about building appropriate relationships with their parents and family members.* Build these discussions into major entry points (such as orientation, move-in weekend, or FYE classes) to educate students on the best ways to include their parents and families in their college lives. Help them develop positive and appropriate relationships *before* those relationships become challenged by an untoward event or a crisis.

NEW DIRECTIONS FOR STUDENT SERVICES • DOI: 10.1002/ss

Programming for parents and family members is an optimal time for staff to partner with them to embrace the positive growth and development of students. Often staff members find their role of programming and outreach for parents and family members in the campus community challenging as they continue to develop new opportunities to appropriately include parents and family members on campus. We believe that engaging parents and families in programming and outreach is well worth the effort. Through these efforts the institution is able to set expectations, define relationships, and involve parents and family members as partners for student success.

References

Austin, D. "The Role of Family Influence on Student Success." In J. A. Ward-Roof and C. Hatch (eds.), *Designing Successful Transitions: A Guide for Orienting Students to College.* Monograph no. 13. Columbia, S.C.: National Resource Center for the First-Year Experience and Students in Transition, 2003.

Coburn, K. L., and Treeger, M. L. *Letting Go: A Parents' Guide to Today's College Experiences.* Bethesda, Md.: Adler and Adler, 1988.

Coburn, K. L., and Treeger, M. L. *Letting Go: A Parents' Guide to Today's College Experiences.* (4th ed.) New York: HarperCollins, 2003.

Cohen, R. D. "From In Loco Parentis to Auxilio Parentum." In R. Cohen (ed.), *Working with Parents of College Students.* New Directions for Student Services, no. 32. San Francisco: Jossey-Bass, 1985.

Hatch, C. "Orienting Nontraditional Students to College: Creating Opportunities, Supporting Success." In J. A. Ward-Roof and C. Hatch (eds.), *Designing Successful Transitions: A Guide for Orienting Students to College.* Monograph no. 13. Columbia, S.C.: National Resource Center for the First-Year Experience and Students in Transition, 2003.

Hurt, J. B., and others. "How Student Affairs Administrators Spend Their Time: Differences by Institutional Setting." *College Student Affairs Journal,* 2003, *23*(1), 7–26.

Jacobs, B. C., and With, E. A. "Orientation's Role in Addressing the Developmental Stages of Parents." *Journal of College Orientation and Transition,* 2002, *9*(2), 37–42.

Merriman, L. S. "Best Practices for Managing Parent Concerns: A Mixed Methods Study of Student Affairs Practice at Doctoral Research Institutions." Unpublished doctoral dissertation, Department of Education, University of California, Los Angeles, 2006.

Mullendore, R. H., and Banahan, L. A. "Channeling Parent Energy and Reaping the Benefits." In K. Keppler, R. H. Mullendore, and A. Carey (eds.), *Partnering with the Parents of Today's College Students.* Washington, D.C.: National Association of Student Personnel Administrators, 2005.

Mullendore, R. H., Banahan, L. A., and Ramsey, J. L. "Developing a Partnership with Today's College Parents." In K. Keppler, R. H. Mullendore, and A. Carey (eds.), *Partnering with the Parents of Today's College Students.* Washington, D.C.: National Association of Student Personnel Administrators, 2005.

Pennington, K. L. "Foreword." In K. Keppler, R. H. Mullendore, and A. Carey (eds.), *Partnering with the Parents of Today's College Students.* Washington, D.C.: National Association of Student Personnel Administrators, 2005.

Strumpf, G. *NODA Databank.* College Park, Md.: National Orientation Directors Association, 2000.

Turrentine, C. G., Schnure, S. L., Ostroth, D., and Ward-Roof, J. A. "The Parent Project: What Parents Want from the College Experience." *NASPA Journal,* 2000, *38*(1), 31–43.

Ward-Roof, J. A. "Parents Orientation: Begin with the End in Mind." In K. Keppler, R. H. Mullendore, and A. Carey (eds.), *Partnering with the Parents of Today's College Stu-*

dents. Washington, D.C.: National Association of Student Personnel Administrators, 2005.

Woollen, S. A. "Influencing Parental Behaviors Through an Orientation Program." *Journal of College Orientation and Transition,* 2005, *12*(2), 80–82.

JEANINE A. WARD-ROOF *is dean of students at Florida State University.*

PATRICK M. HEATON *is assistant dean of students and codirector of new student and family programs at Florida State University.*

MARY B. COBURN *is vice president for student affairs at Florida State University.*

NEW DIRECTIONS FOR STUDENT SERVICES • DOI: 10.1002/ss

5

Parents define student crises every day. Communicating with parents during a crisis and responding to their concerns are critical skills when managing their involvement.

Managing Parent Involvement During Crisis

Lynette S. Merriman

Parents today are not only more involved in their students' lives; they also have a heightened level of concern for their students. Parent concerns range from minor issues like summer storage and parking fines to major crises like suicidal thoughts or an on-campus fire. Regardless of level of concern, the student's well-being is the primary reason parents are contacting university student affairs offices (Merriman, 2007). They also call to resolve an issue, complain, express concern, or share information with administrators.

In the wake of 9/11, Hurricane Katrina, and the Virginia Tech shooting tragedy, it is no surprise that concern for students' safety is the primary reason attributed to parents' increased involvement. Parents and university administrators share in their commitment to student safety. However, college and university staff who assume responsibility for campus crisis management often leave parents out of the information loop when it comes to their crisis plans. Understanding parent expectations during times of crisis, educating both students and families about university support and response efforts, and communicating effectively to families during a crisis situation are all critical to successful crisis management.

This chapter explains the importance of understanding parents when responding to crises, provides an introduction to crisis management, and offers recommendations for assisting families in crisis preparations.

NEW DIRECTIONS FOR STUDENT SERVICES, no. 122, Summer 2008   © Wiley Periodicals, Inc.
Published online in Wiley InterScience (www.interscience.wiley.com) • DOI: 10.1002/ss.275

Campus Crises in Context

The increase in parental involvement across many aspects of higher education has been discussed in several chapters in this volume. However, parental involvement with problem solving and campus crisis presents a greater level of urgency for administrators. Parents are a bit more in tune with campus issues because of the prevailing culture of fear in society overall, as well as technology. As campus administrators assess their crisis and incident responses, they should consider parent involvement in the context of these issues along with the issue of institutional impact.

Culture. One could argue that child safety has always been a priority for this generation of parents. With nanny cams, car seats, bike helmets, toy recalls, and other evidence of child safety concerns, it is no surprise that parents are characterized as overprotective. For college campuses, events such as reports of campus fires that have taken student life, pending pandemic illness, celebratory riots, increased crime, and destructive tornados reinforce the culture of fear for parents of college students. College administrators need to be cognizant of this trend as they respond to parent concerns. When their students live in communities unfamiliar to parents, their fear may further heighten as they realize that the direct assistance they can offer their students has lessened. Additionally, lack of knowledge of an institution's emergency plan and their preparedness can further increase parental anxiety. Empathizing and matching their concern communicates a serious commitment to calming their fears.

Technology. In this age of instant communication—from cell phones to text messages, e-mail, and instant media—the flow of information is continuous, regardless of its accuracy. Parents want to know what is happening in their students' community and will scour every available source for information. Once an event has been identified that could affect the college or their student, concern and panic can ensue.

Furthermore, access to instant information leads to an expectation of instant answers and assistance. Parent web sites invite parents to e-mail directly with questions and concerns. This proactive approach welcomes parent interaction, so parents send e-mails around the clock voicing concern, presenting student issues, and expecting prompt resolution.

Campus administrators need to be aware of incidents or tragedies that happen in their campus neighborhood, regardless of whether the campus is affected or not. Media coverage may lead a parent to believe that a nearby fire, environmental tragedy, or accident has affected their student's campus or, worse yet, their student. When these situations arise, campus frontline responders must be prepared to answer their inquiries quickly and accurately.

Institutional Impact. As Rollo and Zdziarski have observed, "the impact of institutional response over time is profound" (2007, p. 6). During and after large-scale events such as fires, natural disasters, and scandals, the institution will be viewed through a microscope by many, and issues

New Directions for Student Services • DOI: 10.1002/ss

such as preparedness and response will be scrutinized heavily through parent and public lenses. Perception of an institution's response to an event may negatively or positively affect the institution, and the three Rs—reputation, retention, and revenue—are at stake.

Managing reputation is a key component of crisis management. Reputation stems from stakeholder experiences, and positive experiences lead to longevity of trust and confidence. The response to the crisis puts a human face on the institution (Rollo and Zdziarski, 2007, p. 5). If the stakeholders are satisfied with institutional response, they can become ambassadors for the institution. If stakeholders become dissatisfied with institutional response, it can negatively affect the institution's reputation, retention of its students, and possibly revenue. Because satisfied parents may provide additional revenue to the institution and promote it within their communities, they are an "important funding source" (Turrentine, Schnure, Ostroth, and Ward-Roof, 2000, p. 31). Institutions must be cognizant of all of the experiences they provide students and their families, identify and understand their perceptions, and gauge their reactions because these experiences, perceptions, and reactions can affect the institution both positively and negatively.

Defining Crisis

In *Crisis Management: Responding from the Heart,* Gene Zdziarski defines a crisis as "an event, often sudden or unexpected, that disrupts the normal operations of the institution or its educational mission and threatens the well-being of personnel, property, financial resources, and/or reputation of the institution" (2006, p. 5). Crises have always arisen in college environments and, through the lens of campus responders, typically have been defined as negative and disruptive events involving students. This definition implies a broad institutional impact; however, parents are likely to define a crisis from the individual perspective of the student or the family.

Although parents and college administrators recognize that a crisis can occur at many levels, it may be helpful to consider different levels of crisis when creating strategies for working with parents. First, *disasters* affect the institution and the surrounding area. Hurricane Katrina and fires in California requiring institutional evacuation serve as recent examples of disasters. Second, a *crisis* disrupts the operations of the entire campus and may include closure, cancellation of classes, or the need for community gathering. The Virginia Tech shootings, a prolonged campus power outage, the Texas A&M bonfire tragedy, or a fire in an academic building are all clear examples of campus crisis. Third, *critical incidents* affect a smaller portion of the campus: for example, a fraternity house fire, a residential sexual assault, or a fight between student athletes. Any of these incidents can certainly balloon to full-blown crisis (Harper, Paterson, and Zdziarski, 2006). While expectations may vary based on the type of incident, the vast majority of today's parents expect communication.

Although college and university administrators think broadly about campus crisis, parents think more specifically about the health and safety of their student. The basic definition of crisis, "a crucial or decisive point or situation; a turning point," can more easily be applied to the many concerns that parents present today (*American Heritage Dictionary,* 2000, p. 431). A registration hold may prevent students from getting the classes they desire, a failing grade could affect job and graduate school opportunities, a fire in a residence hall greatly disrupts the campus environment and creates multiple issues and concerns that must be addressed, and a campus shooting prompts fear and panic throughout campus communities. From the perspective of a college administrator, the nature of parent concerns range from routine problem solving to critical; however, in the minds of the parent calling on the phone, the concern is already a crisis or is quickly becoming one. Because college administrators' definitions of a crisis may differ from those of parents, one key point must be noted: "a situation becomes a crisis when key stakeholders agree it is a crisis" (Coombs, 1999, p. 89). As stakeholders, parents are defining crisis every day.

Student affairs professionals assume a variety of important roles in managing crises (Siegel, 1991). Crisis management team membership, on-call crisis responsibilities, crisis communication planning, and first responder training are often found in student affairs staff job descriptions. As frontline responders, they have the responsibility to respond to student needs in individual, group, and campuswide crisis situations. With the increased speed of technology, parents have also become frontline responders by phone, web, or even in person. Parents contact numerous campus offices directly, and all administrators need to know how best to interface with them, especially during crisis situations. With parents contacting colleges and universities at a greater rate than ever before, campus responders need listening skills, patience, effective communication skills, and problem-solving skills (Merriman, 2006). Whether working with a parent who has a relatively minor concern or serving as the point person for a major tragedy, communication skills and compassion may be the key criteria when assigning roles to administrators.

Crisis Management

Crisis management is "a process of preventing, preparing for, performing and learning from crises" (Coombs, 1999, p. 5). Crisis literature offers a variety of crisis management plans and models. Plans cannot be rigid and inflexible: crisis is a fluid process that requires a similarly fluid decision-making process. Zdziarski, Rollo, and Dunkel (2007) designed their crisis management model with campuses in mind, and they identify planning, prevention, response, recovery, and learning as steps of the crisis management process. Parents may be involved in each of these steps.

Planning. With parents concerned for the safety of their students, colleges and universities can alleviate some anxiety by proactively educating students and their families about the institution's emergency plan and preparedness. Through written communication, web communication, orientation and parent weekend presentations, and giveaways such as key chains and magnets, families can be informed of emergency protocols and how they can access emergency information. Institutions designate web sites and phone numbers to convey essential information during emergency situations, and it is important that these sites and numbers are widely known and easily accessible.

Openly providing information on evacuation plans, communication plans, and the college or university's support resources and emergency supplies demonstrates to parents that the institution takes emergencies seriously. More important, it demonstrates institutional commitment to the safety and care of their students.

Colleges and universities should also help parents to understand that as a family they can help prepare their student for emergency situations. Institutions should encourage parents to provide their students with one-person survival kits, a family communication plan, and a personal evacuation plan.

Communication plans should include a designated phone number of a family member or friend outside of the campus area. Should city area codes and prefixes get overloaded, this number could serve as a check-in location for the student and their family. Also, it is important that family members are informed that text messages are often the most effective way to communicate during a large-scale emergency. Students and their families should know to look for text messages during critical events and acknowledge their receipt. If there is an event that has a significant impact on the city where the college or university is located, students should know to contact their families and let them know they are safe. Students should also be encouraged to list an ICE number—an in-case-of-emergency number—in their cell phone because it will inform those assisting distressed students of whom to contact should the student become incapacitated.

Families should also be encouraged to identify locations that their student may evacuate to should an evacuation be necessary. These sites may be the home of a relative, family friend, or a roommate or friend of the student. Parents should have the address and phone number for all of these locations. At some institutions prone to environmental disasters such as hurricanes, students are required to develop and submit an evacuation plan to the school.

For an institution's communication plan to be effective it is imperative that students provide their current contact information as well as emergency contact information for their parents should their family need to be notified. Many institutions have emergency notification systems that generate text messages and e-mails to members of the campus community if essential emergency information needs to be disseminated. For such a system to work, it is critical that students provide the school with their up-to-date cell phone numbers. If an institution has an emergency notification system, it would be in their best interest to enable parents to sign up as well.

NEW DIRECTIONS FOR STUDENT SERVICES • DOI: 10.1002/ss

Much about preparing for critical incidents involves conversation. Colleges and universities are well served if they speak with families about emergency preparedness—both expectations of the institution and expectations of the student. These dialogues are in the best interest of all campus stakeholders.

Prevention. Parents can be especially helpful as educators in crisis prevention. A key element to crisis prevention is risk assessment and understanding. For college students, the greatest risks likely include alcohol and other drug misuse and abuse, mental health issues, relationship issues, and academic success. Talking candidly with parents about these issues and how to avoid concerns in these areas will prove beneficial. Empowering parents to create a regular communication plan with their student will also prevent a communication breakdown within the family. Students who don't call home may cause their parents to panic about their welfare. Another important key to prevention with respect to parents is trust. If they trust that the professional staff are being proactive, attentive, and responsive to concerns, critical incidents are less likely to explode into crises.

Response. When in the middle of a critical incident or crisis situation, parents may not be our first focus of concern. However, parents will certainly judge the institution by our responsiveness to them and to their student. For parents, many of whom are involved from a distance, the expeditious communication of critical information is important in demonstrating an institution's effectiveness during a crisis. When a parent arrives on campus, demonstrating care and attentiveness is essential.

Communication. Following the shootings at Virginia Tech, current and prospective parents contacted colleges and universities across the country with their concerns for student safety and wanting to know about the institution's emergency preparedness and crisis management plans. Many institutions had already reviewed and revised student incident protocols and crisis management plans for disaster situations in the aftermath of the 9/11 and Hurricane Katrina tragedies. Now they were addressing how they would protect students and communicate with them and their parents should there be a shooting on campus. According to Blythe (2004), the needs of the stakeholders and how to best meet those needs are essential to a communications protocol. Campuses need to be prepared to respond to parent concerns for any and all crisis situations. They need to anticipate parents' actions and reactions.

Communication should be constant throughout the life cycle of the crisis (Coombs, 1999), and whether it comes via web pages, newsletters, letters, presentations, or conversations, parents today want to be informed (Merriman, 2006). This need for information, coupled with the concern they have for their students' safety, leads to the need for crisis management plans that include a parent communication plan.

Although administrators recognize the parental expectation and need for information, little evidence exists that parents are included in campus crisis communication plans. In a nationwide survey of student affairs professionals who have frequent contact with parents, 21 percent stated that their institution's crisis management plan does not have a communication plan for parents, and 34 percent said they did not know whether such a plan exists. Additionally, 35 percent of the respondents with parent program offices stated that they did not know whether their institutions had a communication plan for parents (Merriman, 2006). In the past decade, American colleges and universities have experienced several large-scale crises that have affected entire campus communities. Even with the recent devastation from hurricane Katrina, the largest natural disaster ever to affect higher education in this country, the data from this study reveal that 55 percent of those surveyed do not appear prepared to respond to parents (Merriman, 2006).

For institutions with numerous out-of-area students, communication during a disaster or crisis is even more essential. However, the same survey mentioned earlier revealed that 28 percent of respondents in institutions with 71 percent or more of their students coming from out of state replied that they do not know whether they have a communication plan for parents in crisis situations. Twenty-five percent of respondents from institutions with 61 to 70 percent out-of-state student populations indicated that their institution does not have a communication plan in place for parents. In the event of a large-scale disaster when an institution is required to evacuate, such as pandemic flu, the logistics for assisting and accommodating these students is challenging. Since parents are unable to assist their students directly, they look to the institution for information and support of their student.

Lack of knowledge about communication plans and the absence of plans indicate that communication with parents during an emergency is not consistently part of the overall planning process. Of the institutions that have a communication plan for parents in their crisis management protocols, 93 percent indicated that parents are directed to the parent web site or university emergency web site for information and instructions. This option was followed by emergency information that would be sent to parents via e-mail (73 percent) and the implementation of a crisis hotline or phone bank (63 percent).

When designing an effective crisis communication plan, knowing the characteristics of the institution's families are important. Understanding language needs and technology ability will maximize communication effectiveness. Depending on the parent population, messages may need to be translated, and phone banks may need to be the dominant form of communication to assist parents who may not have access to the web. Also, in some situations parents will want to speak with a live person.

Parent Support. For some parents, talking with an administrator will successfully resolve their concerns during a crisis. Depending on the crisis, some parents may come to campus to see the situation themselves. A medical emergency, death, assault, or other type of incident may prompt parents to visit the campus. Reflecting on campus response to the suicide of their son, Don and Cathie Klockentager (2006) remind college administrators that "you don't get a second chance to do it right—'it' being how the tragedy is dealt with from initial notification on" (p. 51). Other successful strategies include committing early and genuinely to the crisis, identifying one key point person for all questions from family members, providing opportunities for reflection and grieving, and finding a balance between legal liabilities and compassion (Klockentager and Klockentager, 2006).

In incidents where parents may be notified of their student's serious injury or death, institutions must have a clear process for notification. Parents may not be ready for detailed information, but an expression of care and a campus contact person should be provided.

Recovery and Learning. In these final two stages of the crisis management cycle, parents can provide valuable perspective. During recovery, parents may be in the best position to assess longer-term needs for individual students. Institutions may want to remind parents about campus resources for students who are still processing and reflecting on the incident. A large part of the learning stage is evaluating the management of a crisis, the information provided, and the effectiveness of the communication. Given that parents will be involved in the crisis, even from a distance, it seems logical that they will have an opinion on how improvements can be made. Using a parent advisory board or the parent association as a starting point is efficient and practical. A web survey in a parent e-newsletter may also be effective.

Responding to Individual Student Crisis or Problem-Solving Needs

So far, the crisis management steps discussed here have related to large-scale disaster, crisis, or critical incidents. However, some crises occur at the individual level, such as those involving health, academics, personal challenges, or family issues. Individual crises include a student who experiences the death of a grandparent, the divorce of parents, a low grade in a course, violation of campus policies, or a disease like mononucleosis. These issues range from routine problem-solving concerns (like low grades and the flu) to more serious personal concerns such as divorce or a judicial matter that may end in suspension. When parents intervene in these crisis situations, some of the same principles apply.

Provide information and parenting guidance. Parents are looking primarily for advice and information. As will be discussed in Chapter Seven of this volume, college staff may be prohibited from sharing personal information because of student privacy laws (Family Educational Rights and Privacy Act, or FERPA) and health record confidentiality (Health Insurance Portability and Accountability Act, or HIPAA). However, administrators can always share process and resource information. Arming parents with knowledge and resources can diffuse a personal crisis.

One of the more difficult questions for campus administrators is whether parents should come to campus. On one hand, the student is the adult problem solver; however, in times of crisis, parental support may be necessary. College administrators should not be afraid to answer this question. If the parent is not needed, responding in a way that affirms the student's ability to handle the situation independently is appropriate. If the parent's presence would be helpful (in cases of hospitalization or impending suspension, for instance), answer candidly that the student would benefit from parent support.

Consider emergency notification protocols carefully. Although parents often initiate contact, there may be times when crisis notification is appropriate, and the process and boundaries must be carefully considered. In a survey of doctoral research institutions, the majority of respondents stated that the decision to notify parents depended on the severity of the incident for individual crises such as alcohol violations, emergency room visits, and attempted suicides. Only in cases of attempted suicides at private institutions did a small majority of 51 percent state that parents are notified (Merriman, 2006). Parental notification will be more fully explored in Chapter Seven on legal responsibilities.

Conclusion

Parents today are increasingly involved because they are concerned about their student. As college campuses experience crises, these events are being broadcast for all parents to see, analyze, judge, and more commonly question. Parents want to know how their student's institution will respond to such an event, and feel confident—as much as they can—that their student's college or university is prepared to take care of their student should a crisis arise.

Colleges and universities should explain their crisis management plans to parents, their communication plans, their notification policies, and how to access this information. Institutions also are better served if they proactively assist families in preparing their own emergency plans and help them to understand what the institution expects of them during a critical event.

Overall, the diversity of parents and families needs to be considered when responding to concerns and issues. Because of the ethnic diversity of college students, language barriers may require special thought and accommodation, especially during a crisis. Families may also approach crisis differently, with some seeking assistance openly and others demanding privacy and isolation. Divorced parents present another challenge for crisis communication. Which parent is contacted in an emergency or crisis? Can both parents be contacted? Finally, the geographic distance between students and parents may create special considerations for crisis planning. Physical distance may create an emotional distance that is difficult to read during a crisis. Parents may overreact or underreact to an incident. For example, the parents of a student who attempted suicide may choose not to come to campus after the student downplays the seriousness of the attempt. Careful planning for these unique needs of parents and students will strengthen crisis response plans.

NEW DIRECTIONS FOR STUDENT SERVICES • DOI: 10.1002/ss

According to Sandeen, "an institution reveals its soul during a crisis" (2006). Whether working with students or parents, an institution's responsiveness reflects its campus culture of care, inclusion, and community. Including parents as members of the campus community during a crisis creates effective lifelong partnerships.

References

American Heritage Dictionary. (4th ed.) Boston: Houghton Mifflin, 2000.

Blythe, B. T. "The Human Side of Crisis Management."

Coombs, W. T. *Ongoing Crisis Communication: Planning, Managing, and Responding.* Thousand Oaks: Sage Publications, 1999.

Harper, K. S., Paterson, B. G., and Zdziarski, E. L. (eds.). *Crisis Management: Responding from the Heart.* Washington, D.C.: National Association of Student Personnel Administrators, 2006.

Klockentager, D., and Klockentager, C. "Voice of the Parents." In K. S. Harper, B. G. Paterson, and E. L. Zdziarski (eds.), *Crisis Management: Responding from the Heart.* Washington, D.C.: National Association of Student Personnel Administrators, 2006.

Merriman, L. S. "Best Practices for Managing Parent Concerns: A Mixed Methods Study of Student Affairs Practice at Doctoral Research Institutions." Doctoral dissertation, University of California, Los Angeles, 2006.

Merriman, L. S. "Managing Parental Involvement." *NASPA Leadership Exchange,* 2007, 5(1), 14–18.

Mitroff, I. I. *Stakeholders of the Organizational Mind.* San Francisco: Jossey-Bass Publishers, 1983.

Rollo, J. M., and Zdziarski II, E. L. "The Impact of Crisis." In E. L. Zdziarski II, N. W. Dunkel, J. M. Rollo, and Associates (eds.), *Campus Crisis Management.* San Francisco: Jossey-Bass, 2007.

Sandeen, A. "Voice of the Vice President." In K. S. Harper, B. G. Paterson, and E. L. Zdziarski (eds.), *Crisis Management: Responding from the Heart.* Washington, D.C.: National Association of Student Personnel Administrators, 2006.

Siegel, D. G. "Crisis Management: The Campus Responds." *Educational Record,* 1991, 72(3), 14–16.

Turrentine, C. G., Schnure, S. L., Ostroth, D. D., and Ward-Roof, J. A. "The Parent Project: What Parents Want from the College Experience." *NASPA Journal,* 2000, 38(1), 31–43.

Zdziarski, E. L. "Crisis in the Context of Higher Education." In K. S. Harper, B. G. Paterson, and E. L. Zdziarski (eds.), *Crisis Management: Responding from the Heart.* Washington, D.C.: National Association of Student Personnel Administrators, 2006.

Zdziarski II, E. L, Rollo, J. N., and Dunkel, N. W. "The Crisis Matrix." In E. L. Zdziarski II, N. W. Dunkel, J. M. Rollo, and Associates (eds.), *Campus Crisis Management.* San Francisco: Jossey-Bass, 2007.

LYNETTE S. MERRIMAN is the senior associate dean for student affairs at the University of Southern California.

6

Given the time and energy that student affairs administrators currently devote to parents, thoughtful needs assessment, development of a clear philosophy, and identification of resources are critical to the success of outreach efforts.

Developing, Staffing, and Assessing Parent Programs

Marjorie Savage

The growing consensus in higher education, and what this volume illustrates, is that today's mothers and fathers are closely involved with their student during the college years. When administrators consider the process of defining that role, developing a new parent program, or assessing an existing one, important steps include considering the institution's philosophy on working with family members, determining placement of services within the institution, and selecting the right staff to work with parents.

Philosophical Considerations

As colleges and universities adjust to the changing relationship between today's students and their families, the benefits of providing parent services become increasingly clear. Parents have a stake in their student's education because of the financial and personal investment they are making. Today's young adults are in frequent contact—50 percent of eighteen- to twenty-five-year-olds say they are in touch with parents daily (Pew Research Center for the People and the Press, 2007)—and three-quarters of students say they follow their parents' advice (National Survey of Student Engagement, 2007). If the college or university can guide that care, concern, and advice, parents are potentially our best allies in student development and retention efforts. They also may be a source of funding for overextended higher education budgets.

New Directions for Student Services, no. 122, Summer 2008 © Wiley Periodicals, Inc.
Published online in Wiley InterScience (www.interscience.wiley.com) • DOI: 10.1002/ss.276

The key to developing successful services and using parent interest productively is to focus on *appropriate* involvement. What that means, though, can be very different depending on an institution's mission and goals, the profile of the school's students, the cost of attending, and even the size of the campus. Appropriate parent involvement may be different for commuter students than for residential students or for students with a disability. What works well at one school or for one population segment might turn out to be a poor choice for another.

In the field of parent services, there are two basic models that have proven successful: the "student development" model and the "financial development" model. From a student affairs perspective, a parent program will establish parent services that are founded on goals for student success. When parents are seeking information about or accommodations for their student, a student development response would consider what's best for the student, how that relates to what's best for students in general, and how the student can take ownership of the issue. As an example, consider the parent who fears that his daughter's roommate is inviting friends into the room every night, disturbing his daughter's studying and sleep, and he wants the roommate moved out. With a student development model, the response might be a recommendation that the roommates discuss and come to an agreement on visiting hours. It may include an offer for a staff member to mediate a discussion and an explanation of the room transfer process. It may note that a student would not be removed from a room based on a third-party complaint, and that the policy requires documentation of a violation before a student would be moved or asked to leave the hall. It may suggest that the daughter has the option of requesting a room change for herself but not for her roommate and explain how the daughter can make that request. Parent involvement under this model relies on parents understanding and supporting the institutional processes and developmental goals of the college or university.

With the financial development model, the institution's primary goal in working with parents is to cultivate them as donors, to recognize them as a customer (as the payer of tuition), or to attract or maintain them as friends of the college or university. Here, parents' requests (or at least *some* parents' requests) might require finding a positive response. To use the same example as above, if the parent has an influential role in the community, is in a position to make a significant donation to the institution, or is likely to pursue the request to increasingly higher authorities, the daughter's roommate may be relocated, or the daughter may be given a new, better housing assignment. This approach requires an across-the-board understanding of when policies can be bent, and it can result in tension between institutional rules and institutional relationships.

When the college or university clearly identifies that underlying philosophy for parent services, staff can work with parents' requests. Often the goals of working with parents encompass both philosophies—student development *and* institutional advancement—or the goals may change depending on the parents involved. When the goals are unclear or are frequently changing, the conflict between rules and relationships can create significant confusion. From the staff point of view, parents become the enemy and are viewed as a problem if it is unclear when to cite policy and procedure and when to find a way to say yes despite standard operating procedures.

Parent programs usually start with a perceived need or a perceived benefit. Whether the parent program focuses on student development or advancement typically depends on who first identifies a need for the program. When a program is conceived in a student affairs office, the perceived need is likely to be driven by parents articulating their expectations for services and information or by a recognition that students are relying on parents for assistance in solving problems. In some cases, student development–based programs have been born out of frustration that parents are showing up for student orientation, dropping into student advising sessions, or calling housing staff for updates on their student. Other schools began their parent programs because students were pulling out their cell phones to call parents during counseling appointments or in the midst of an orientation workshop. Schools are increasingly acknowledging that by giving parents accurate and timely information, the family can refer their student to the appropriate resources at the appropriate time or can reinforce the messages that campus staff gives students. The benefit, then, is that with parents' help students will begin to understand their own responsibilities and abilities while also receiving appropriate assistance when they most need it.

For a fundraising office, the perceived need is financial, and the benefit is that parents become willing donors when they can see that their gifts provide direct support to their students. Parents will contribute to a campus safety effort, library fund, or late-night programming efforts when they see how those projects can positively affect students like theirs.

In 2007, more than half of parent programs nationally were housed in a student affairs or student development office, and another quarter of parent services fell under the direction of a fundraising or advancement office (Savage, 2007). The remaining programs were scattered among alumni offices, academic affairs, public relations, enrollment management, direct report to the president, or a dual reporting line to a combination of offices. With an understanding of the institution's philosophy and goals for working with family members, it becomes more apparent where the office should report and who will be the key people determining how parent services will be established.

Review Campus Culture. The term *campus culture* is often used loosely, with trust that everyone knows what it means, but this phrase is hard to pin down. Truthfully, there is rarely just one campus culture. A school's history department will probably have an entirely different culture from the computer technology department. The culture surrounding athletic events will be very different from that of the same institution's music or theater events.

NEW DIRECTIONS FOR STUDENT SERVICES • DOI: 10.1002/ss

At the same time, though, there are some overarching attitudes, outlooks, values, and expectations that characterize an institution, its philosophies, and structures. Private and public schools have some inherent differences. The messages given to prospective students, the level of tolerance considered acceptable for different behaviors, the kind of annual events the school sponsors—these all reflect institutional culture. Private colleges and universities are more likely to house parent services in a fundraising office (41 percent), whereas public colleges and universities more often include parent services as part of student affairs (71 percent).

When we are defining campus culture, institutional characteristics and descriptors—such as urban, rural, faith-based, community-focused, service-oriented, political, or research-focused—often come to mind first. However, those same descriptors may be less helpful when assessing the needs of and providing services for parents. Given institutional cultural definition and parent characteristics, will parents feel comfortable on campus? For example, if campus culture is fairly activist oriented but your families are not, there may be some difficulties with trust and understanding.

Additionally, students may embrace the campus cultural values and norms, but those values may conflict with family perspectives. If the institution's culture reflects a strong social justice orientation, students may go home at breaks to a home less tolerant than the campus environment. On the other hand, parents may be fully accepting of the campus culture and hope to participate in campus rituals and traditions (Adams, Downey, and Roccaforte, 2005).

Assess Campus Messages for Consistency. Whether an institution has a formal parent program or not, messages are being delivered to parents, and parents notice when they receive inconsistent messages from their student's college or university. A critical step in working with families is to assemble all the messages being communicated by all the offices on campus and ensure that they are relevant, accurate, and congruent. Parents will be disappointed, irritated, or angry if the promises they have received are not delivered. Many parents receive their first in-person introduction to the college or university through the admissions office, when they are given a sense—correct or not—of what kind of students attend, the academic rigor and educational approach, and the values of the campus community. Those initial expectations must be accurate from the beginning and consistent as the school continues to communicate with families beyond the admissions process and as parent services, activities, and events are developed and delivered.

From a marketing standpoint, the admissions office wants to promote the best possible image of safety, academic excellence, quality teaching, small classes, and contemporary facilities. Tours for prospective students and their parents highlight examples of those positive markers. But are first-year students then assigned to the oldest residence halls? Are they expected to sign up for the largest lecture courses, where most of their faculty contact will be with a teaching assistant? Are they subjected to less-than-ideal safety and security conditions when they step beyond the boundaries of the campus? Parents are looking for evidence that their students are receiving the services and opportunities they were promised.

These expectations apply to the style, quality, and level of the treatment parents themselves receive as well, and delivery of those promises requires collaboration across campus and through the years. For example, if parents have been warmly welcomed during the college selection process, they will have expectations that their student is attending a family-friendly school. They will anticipate that their presence on campus will be encouraged. Admissions events for prospective students and their parents featuring the 360-member marching band, indoor fireworks, and a talk by the president should be followed throughout the college years by a similar level of grandeur and welcome at Parent-Family weekend, homecoming events, and commencement ceremonies. If communications are free-flowing and open throughout the application and admissions phase, there will be an expectation that communications will continue in the same spirit when the student arrives on campus. The Family Educational Rights and Privacy Act (FERPA), then, can come as a rude awakening unless the institution clearly explains the change that occurs with matriculation.

Family expectations are also influenced by the perceived investment the school makes to recruit their student. If a school's recruitment materials and processes have been high tech and high quality, parents will continue to expect these standards in their continuing experience. A parent whose son attended a highly competitive, prestigious, private college reported that before her son committed to the school, every piece of information the family received was very professional, collegiate looking, and impressive. But when she went to the school's parent orientation, she was given a parent handbook—a rather shabby publication, dotted with typos, illustrated with cartoonish graphics rather than photos, and bound with a plastic spiral binding. "It was really kind of 'low rent,'" she said. It made her feel first that parents were not highly regarded by the school, and then she also wondered, If they're putting all their funds into marketing, will they actually follow through with my son beyond the admissions phase? (confidential personal communication with parent, July 23, 2005).

Develop a Mission Statement. Parent services should be guided by a mission statement that reflects the institutional and departmental philosophy and vision for working with parents. Development of programs and services should evolve from the mission and vision to meet the purpose of the program. The mission statement will be different depending on the kind of institution, the reporting structure for the proposed parent services, and the goals that have been identified for working with parents.

NEW DIRECTIONS FOR STUDENT SERVICES • DOI: 10.1002/ss

For example, Augsburg College, a small, private, faith-based college in Minneapolis, Minnesota, includes parent services in its office for institutional advancement. The mission of the Augsburg parent program is

> "to facilitate communication between parents/families and the College in order to develop and nurture meaningful, lasting relationships between Augsburg College and our parents and families" (Sally Daniels, personal communication, June 11, 2007).

Hope College, another small, private, faith-based school, combines parent services with the alumni program and has a strong fundraising goal. The mission statement reads as follows:

> The mission of the Hope College Parent Relations program is to:
> - Facilitate communication between parents and the College
> - Develop and nurture meaningful, lasting relationships between parents and the College
> - Sponsor programs and services that will engage parents in the life of the College and endear them to the College's mission
> - Promote the development of the College and its students by encouraging parental support of the Hope Fund and other financial projects [Savage, 2005, p. 26]

At Western Washington University, a midsized public university, parent services are part of student affairs, and the parent program is combined with new student services. The mission statement clearly reflects a focus on the college transition phase of student development:

> "New Student Services/Family Outreach fosters student learning and development by supporting new students and family members in their transition to the academic, personal, and social experience of WWU" (Savage, 2005, p. 29).

Johnson & Wales University, a midsized, private university in Providence, Rhode Island, also houses its parent program in the student affairs office. Their mission statement both defines the goals of the program and assigns a role for parents. "Parents' Association Mission Statement: the program is the primary link between parents, their students, and the university community. Through important programs and initiatives, the Association connects parents to other parents to provide support, creates a forum for their ideas and opinions, and recognizes they are a valuable resource within the university" (Savage, 2005, p. 26).

Practical Considerations

Once a clear philosophy has been identified, institutional messages checked for consistency, and a mission statement developed, it is logical to then begin exploring functional considerations, such as program funding, staffing, and services and activities.

Determine Funding. In an era of tight budgets and increasing demand for every dollar, it may seem impossible to fund a new parent program. Budget, however, need not be the prohibitive factor. Few parent programs have large budgets, and many are self-supporting.

Funds come from a range of sources: special initiative grants to support program start-up, an annual funding line in institutional or departmental budgets, membership fees from parent members, funds raised through an advancement program, or a self-supported budget raised through program fees for orientation, parents weekend, or newsletter subscriptions. In many cases, parent budgets combine contributions from two or more of these sources. Although the majority of programs indicated that they received at least some of their budget through institutional budgeting, about 20 percent do not receive any central funding; instead they fund their programs through membership fees, parent donations, or event and activity fees. While the first few years of parent services may require an investment of start-up funds from the institution, it's possible to plan for a reduced or self-funded program down the road.

How much does it cost to support a parent office? Comparing budgets is like comparing apples to oranges to fruit salad. Nearly a quarter of programs have an operating budget of $10,000 or less (excluding salary and benefits, which will be discussed under staffing needs). Some have no allocated budget and are self-funded by event or membership fees. At the other extreme are programs with more than $300,000 (Savage, 2007); these are usually combined with an alumni, advancement office, orientation program, or new student programs budget.

Consider Staffing. The background, skills, and interests of the person or people selected to work with parents are closely tied to the types of services the institution will be able to provide, the flavor of the program, and the success of the effort. If fundraising is to be a central component of the program, obviously the right person for the job is a skilled and motivated fundraiser. If the major focus of the program is on delivering a parent orientation program, a background in orientation or first-year experience will be needed. With a trend moving toward combining student development and institutional advancement, the term "generalist" increasingly defines parent program staff. When asked what previous experience had been most helpful as preparation for working with parents, program professionals came up with a lengthy list: communications, public relations, knowledge of student development, teaching, fundraising, event planning, counseling, customer service, and having been a parent—particularly having parented a college-age student (Savage, 2007).

In addition to professional skills, however, there are some purely personal skills that also make a difference. Parent program staff said their most useful attributes are listening skills, communication skills, problem-solving ability, and patience (Merriman, 2006).

For most parent program staff, parent services represent a minor portion of their job responsibilities. Only about a quarter of parent staff nationally are assigned full-time to a parent-family program. Other combined or collateral assignments include "institutional giving," campus activities, orientation, alumni association, retention, external relations, special projects, church relations, and assistance to the chief student affairs officer.

The salary range of parent program staff is as varied as professional backgrounds and titles. The median salary falls in the range of $50,000 to $59,000 per year, but there is variation depending on experience in higher education, educational level, reporting structure of the position, and whether the institution is private or public. For example, more parent program staff in public institutions have a master's degree or higher (68.9 percent in public colleges and universities, compared to about 50 percent in private institutions). Those public institution staff members are less likely to receive a salary of $60,000 or more, however. About a quarter of the parent program staff at public institutions earned $60,000 or more, while just over 40 percent of those at private institutions fell into the $60,000-plus categories (Savage, 2007).

Although a handful of parent staff at both publics and privates receive $30,000 or less, those individuals typically are working with the program at a rate of twenty hours per week or less. The very few who work full-time and receive $30,000 or less have graduate assistantships for their position. At the other end of the spectrum, the respondents who are earning $80,000 or more typically are directors of an annual fund or are senior student affairs officers whose work with parents is just one part of their responsibilities (Savage, 2007).

Determine Services and Activities. In accord with the mission and goals of the institution, funds available, and skills of the staff, priorities can be established on the types of services and activities the office will provide. Earlier chapters described in detail some of the most common parent events and services, but not all schools decide to—or need to—provide all the possible services. In terms of program delivery, student affairs professionals broadly describe four methods for effectively responding to parent concerns: information (resources and issues they can expect to face); programs (informational programs, events on campus, and opportunities for interaction with administrators); parent councils, advisory groups, or boards; and access to student records (Merriman, 2006).

More specifically, nearly every college and university parent program provides four basic services: a parent orientation program, a parent-family weekend, a web site for parents, and e-mail responses to parent questions. In addition to these four, the majority of schools solicit funds from parents (85.2 percent), provide a parent handbook (79 percent), organize parent events on residence hall move-in day (74 percent), and publish an e-mail newsletter for parents (73 percent) (Savage, 2007).

For a new program or for one that is reviewing its priorities, determining services and events includes consideration of which activities are most critical and serve as building blocks for future services. A consistent message from parent program staff is "Don't try to do everything at once. Prioritize. Pick one or two new projects a year and do them well. Be sure you have time and resources before adding anything else" (Savage, 2007).

Assessing Parent Services

When a college or university knows who its parents are, what their relationship is to their students, and what issues they are concerned about, the institution will be able to develop services that meet the needs of students, parents, and the institution. As a program moves forward, those needs will likely change. The services the program provides today are not the services it should be providing in five years. Just as families are continually changing, the needs and expectations of college parents are also changing. Programs and services that don't meet expectations should be revised or replaced. Better parent relations may lead to new programming or new involvement opportunities. Emerging technology or a campus crisis can drive a demand for something more or different.

A foundational benchmark followed by a regular system of assessment and evaluation provides information on what's working, what's not, what else is needed, and perhaps where to cut services and save money. Equally important, benchmarking can identify any population segments that are not being reached or that are reacting differently to programs, services, and messages. For example, it's possible that parents who did not themselves attend college are less likely to attend parent orientation, less likely to subscribe to online parent newsletters, or less likely to read college-identified mail that comes to their home. Thus, more personal forms of outreach may be needed for the families of first-generation students to help them understand the campus resources and services available to their student and to the parents themselves.

Continue Assessment of Programs and Services. We often think of assessment as a formal, lengthy research project, which can seem intimidating and time-consuming. Simply figuring out where to start can feel like a huge undertaking. Valuable parent input can come in different forms, though.

Focus groups and polls. A few focus groups—small, information-gathering conversations guided by a facilitator—allow participants to simply talk about what they want, how they use the information they're receiving, what their needs are, and when they need different kinds of services. Although they do not provide statistically significant information, focus groups provide insights and perspectives that help colleges and universities understand their parents better. While focus groups with parents can give insights on how best to communicate with them, what topics to discuss, and what issues are most important at what times of the academic cycle, focus groups with students can also provide valuable insights. Bringing together a group of students of color, commuters, or first-generation students can reduce the guesswork and give concrete ideas on the topics they want their parents to know more about and the best ways to reach them.

A simple online poll posted on the parent web site each month can provide feedback on issues parents are thinking about and also make the web site more interactive and interesting. The information from a poll can indicate changes over time and to the demographics of parents who use your web site. Several schools have asked parents such questions as "What has been your greatest concern for your student this year?" Sample responses included academics, health and safety, finances, career planning, campus involvement, time management, personal relationships, and an open-ended selection, "other." Schools have also asked how often parents are communicating with their student, what percentage of college expenses the student is expected to contribute, and the simple question, "How old are you?" Neither focus groups nor polls yield statistically significant data, but they do provide helpful information that may guide future assessment and decision making.

Daily logs. Useful data can be gleaned from everyday interactions with parents. Web tracking software shows which pages of a parent web site are being visited. A spreadsheet noting the questions that come in throughout the year offers valuable information about topics of concern to parents and the seasonal timing of different issues. Notations on parent questions can include the date, general topic, specific question, the institution's response, and—to the extent that the information is available—the student's gender and year in school and the gender of the parent. By including those last items—student's year in school and gender—the parent program can determine which issues are most notable for students through the academic cycle and identify whether parents worry more about their sons or their daughters, and which parent is most likely to make the phone call.

By keeping track of calls and looking for trends over the course of a year, a parent program can respond proactively to issues that are likely to come up at different times in the academic cycle. If the same question is being asked multiple times in a week, the question and answer can be sent out to all parents, reducing the number of times an office has to address that issue individually.

Evaluation forms. One of the most frequently used assessment tools is the program evaluation. At the end of a parent orientation program, for example, parents are asked to fill out an evaluation form. The information gleaned from evaluations can be helpful in planning for future events, but the real value comes from knowing whether parents gained knowledge from the program and if they can specify how they will use the information.

Maybe most important, follow-up questions at a later date can determine whether the knowledge was retained and used.

Benchmark and longitudinal surveys. Formal surveys take time and thought, but they provide the evidence to justify services, plan a budget, and improve the program. For parent program staff to do their work on a daily basis and in order to talk with campus colleagues and supervisors about parents, they must know who the parents are, what their relationship is with their students, what their concerns are, whether and how they use the information they receive, and whether they need additional services. (See Appendix A for sample survey questions.) It also helps to know how peer institutions are providing parent services and how those trends are shaping parents' expectations.

Over time and with repeated surveys, the program will be able to collect evidence to determine if changes are being seen. Are parents using the services provided? Have behaviors changed, such as patterns of parent-student contact or attendance at campus events? Are parents more likely to feel connected to and satisfied with the institution?

Including demographic information in a survey allows the institution to determine whether the parent program—and the survey—is reaching all potential parent audiences. By comparing data with institutional racial and cultural records, the survey can show whether respondents reflect the diversity of the students. A question about where the student is living will reveal whether parents of commuters are attending orientation, using parent services, and responding to the survey at a level comparable to your student commuter population. A question about the parent's educational background can determine whether parents of first-generation students are receiving and responding to your communications and services as well as to your surveys.

Use the Data. Parents are investing heavily in their student's institution, sending not only their tuition dollars but, more importantly, their student. With such strong ties to the school, they are happy to provide feedback, and they want to know the college or university will use that information. After evaluating the data, it is important to let them know it is being used.

Survey results can help parents understand what's typical and normal. When parents hear they are not the only parents communicating daily with their student, it is confirmation that they are not "wrong" to do so. They will be relieved to hear that the school recognizes their concerns about health and safety. They opt to wait rather than call with questions about billing dates or grade postings if they trust the institution will give them the information they need when it is most timely. They appreciate hearing the outcome of survey findings—perhaps their frustration with FERPA restrictions has led to an easier information release process for students to give access to grades and financial statements. When parents know the institution has asked, listened, and responded, they feel their time and opinions are valued.

NEW DIRECTIONS FOR STUDENT SERVICES • DOI: 10.1002/ss

Assessment information gathered by a parent program can be helpful not only to the program itself, but also to colleagues across campus. When a survey finds evidence, for instance, that parents routinely talk to their students about career fairs and internship possibilities, career advisers are more likely to see value in developing parent workshops designed to help parents distinguish an appropriate role for family members from an inappropriate one as they work with their student on career topics.

Similarly, the orientation staff should know whether those who attended parent orientation are more satisfied with their student's college experience or more likely than nonattendees to trust their student to manage the campus experience—for example, University of Minnesota data indicated that parents who attend orientation communicate less frequently with their student throughout the year, and they come to campus less often to visit their student (Savage and Pierce, 2006). The orientation office also gains insights from surveys by looking at parents' reasons for deciding not to attend orientation: "I attended the university twenty years ago"; "I attended an orientation when my older child started college"; "My student will be living at home, not in a residence hall"; or "The program is too expensive." These reasons can be addressed in invitations to encourage parents to attend orientation to see what the college experience is like now, compared to twenty years ago; to consider the campus experience for *this* student; to address specific issues for commuter students; and to apply for a scholarship to help fund the parent orientation program.

When a survey indicates that parents are looking for services the institution does not provide, how critical is it to respond with new services? A review of the original mission of the program should confirm or challenge whether the program is fulfilling the purposes under which it was established. Would adding a new service benefit students and parents or lend itself to improving fundraising efforts? If it makes sense and is affordable, it might be worth considering. On the other hand, if a new service would be cost-prohibitive or would not fit the mission of the program, parent pressure should not force the institution to provide it.

Assessment allows a school to assess its own practices and also to compare data with comparable institutions. If one school is including parents in decision making, communicating frequently, and using parents as volunteers at admissions events, that precedent may establish expectations for its peer institutions. Benchmarking with peer institutions may also help build a case for additional resources; however, it is important not to assume a program is failing if it looks different from the parent program at another institution. If the program is based on institutional values and culture, reflects the mission statement's goals in working with parents, is staffed properly, and parents indicate that they are satisfied, the program will meet the needs of the institution's students and their parents.

Certainly assessment data are useful when considering budget and staffing increases. Data indicating that three-fourths of parents have signed up for the e-mail listserv or evidence that more parents are attending on-campus programs show that the interest in parent services is real. A report showing that 90 percent of parents are using the parent program's messages when they talk with their students provides a powerful indication that there is value in parent communications.

Conclusion

All the evidence, from research studies to observations on campus, indicates that parents and students today are closely connected. Parents have influence over their students, and they can be a valuable resource in working on the institution's goals for student development, retention, and graduation. As institutions have sought to work with this family constituency, parent services have frequently developed piecemeal and in decentralized forms. The orientation office may see a need for a parent orientation session and put together a program; the advancement office may identify parents as a new group of donors; the alumni office might determine that families would be a good audience for homecoming; the registrar's office will decide they need to explain FERPA restrictions. With or without a parent program, it's clear that parent messages will be communicated from multiple departments. Colleges and universities can practice effective, positive parent relations by determining an appropriate institutional philosophy on parent involvement, delivering consistent messages, and meeting the multifaceted needs of students, parents, and the college or university.

References

Adams, S., Downey, J., and Roccaforte, M. "Incorporating the HLC Self-Study into Your Campus Culture." Paper presented at Higher Learning Commission annual meeting, Phoenix, Ariz., April 9, 2005. Retrieved Jan. 4, 2008, from www.ncahlc.org/download/annualmeeting/05Handouts/S106_107i_Roccaforte.pdf.

Merriman, L. S. "Best Practices for Managing Parent Concerns: A Mixed Methods Study of Student Affairs Practice at Doctoral Research Institutions." Doctoral dissertation, University of California, Los Angeles, 2006.

National Survey of Student Engagement. "Experiences That Matter: Enhancing Student Learning and Success." Bloomington, Ind.: National Survey of Student Engagement, 2007.

Pew Research Center for the People and the Press. "A Portrait of 'Generation Next: How Young People View Their Lives, Futures and Politics.'" Washington, D.C.: Pew Research Center for the People and the Press, 2007.

Savage, M. "National Survey of College and University Parent Programs." Minneapolis: University of Minnesota, 2005.

Savage, M. "National Parent Program Survey." Minneapolis: University of Minnesota, 2007.

Savage, M., and Pierce, M. J. "University Parent Survey 2006." Minneapolis: University of Minnesota, 2006.

MARJORIE SAVAGE is the parent program director at the University of Minnesota Twin Cities.

7

*This chapter describes the relationship between federal
student privacy laws and state privacy laws, and identifies the changes in the federal law over the last ten years
affecting disclosure to parents of college students. Recent
litigation on health emergencies is outlined and the
limited rights of college students not yet eighteen years
of age are examined.*

Navigating State and Federal Student Privacy Laws to Design Educationally Sound Parental Notice Policies

Thomas R. Baker

Since 1998, the federal law governing student education records has
changed considerably. Appeals courts recently confirmed the primacy of the
Family Education Rights and Privacy Act of 1974 (FERPA) when federal law
conflicts with state law, and the U.S. Supreme Court handed down a ruling
in a FERPA case for the first time in history. Meanwhile, Congress took
action to amend FERPA, and U.S. Department of Education (DE) officials
issued a number of novel statements to clarify the original language of
FERPA. Many of the latest rulings and new laws are designed to facilitate
communication with parents of college students with or without the consent of the students. The tragic murders at Virginia Tech in 2007 precipi-
tated a flurry of public statements clarifying the boundaries of FERPA as
well as a nationwide exploration of the value of parent involvement in the
lives of college-age children. As a whole, the DE correspondence issued
since 1999 provides invaluable assistance in understanding such practical
matters as the use of electronic signatures, the definition of parent, the
health and safety emergency exception, the limits of the rule against redisclosure, and the proper means for confirming a student's dependency financial status.

Currently, notice to parents is neither prohibited nor mandated by law.
On those campuses that view parental notice as an educationally sound
practice, FERPA provides administrators with several means to disclose

NEW DIRECTIONS FOR STUDENT SERVICES, no. 122, Summer 2008 © Wiley Periodicals, Inc.
Published online in Wiley InterScience (www.interscience.wiley.com) • DOI: 10.1002/ss.277

education record information to parents. As more families acquire the technology necessary to access the Internet and e-mail, parents are able to obtain academic information without assistance from college administrators. However, with federal law becoming less restrictive, state restrictions on information disclosure may control the day-to-day practice of student affairs administration. As long as state laws governing education records also permit parental notice, university administrators have considerable discretion to communicate with parents by using the federal privacy law exceptions.

The Universe of State Laws and Federal Laws

To understand the relationship between parents and students, one must consider when a child becomes an adult. The defining age for adulthood is eighteen, although some states complicate matters through restrictions on gambling, handgun purchases, and alcohol possession until twenty-one. When children become adults, they accept responsibility for their choices and are given sole access to their educational and health records. Fortunately for university administrators, the age of majority coincides approximately with high school graduation. Although some university administrators refer to traditional-age college students as "postadolescent pre-adults" in terms of developmental level (Pavela, 1992), American jurisprudence currently recognizes no such legal category between adults and minors.

In most, if not all, states an eighteen-year-old can give consent to medical treatment, establish legal residence apart from the parents, and declare financial independence from the parents (Kaplin and Lee, 2006). With regard to business transactions, an institution can legally enforce a contract signed by an eighteen-year-old without the need for a cosigner. The eighteen-year-old student in turn is entitled to enforce his or her contract rights in court. The adult student's rights take precedent even when a parent is involved.

For the most part, states define the rights of adults and delineate the legal relationship between adult students and parents. State law provides guidance for educational records; however, the federal legislation of FERPA sets the national standard for educational records. When state and federal laws differ, the law that provides greater privacy for the student prevails. Consequently, state law may prohibit university administrators from disclosing information to parents, even though disclosure is not prohibited by FERPA.

Educational records laws, primarily through FERPA, provide the boundaries for disclosure to parents about student grades, progress, and disciplinary issues. Although the legal status of persons age eighteen to twenty under state law may vary somewhat, FERPA protects every postsecondary student attending a federally funded university.

States also provide guidance on disclosure and access to student records and the administrative policies for these issues (Kaplin and Lee, 2006). Disclosure often requires express permission, and students have broad access

NEW DIRECTIONS FOR STUDENT SERVICES • DOI: 10.1002/ss

to personal education records. When education administrators violate the state's privacy law, the student may be entitled under state law to file a lawsuit or submit a formal complaint to the regulatory agency responsible for enforcing state education policy. Private universities in some jurisdictions are governed by the same state privacy laws that regulate student records at public universities.

Federal regulations regarding educational records stem from FERPA. In order to protect fully the privacy rights of adult students, Congress in 1974 terminated parent access rights to the child's education records once the child entered college. The reluctance of Congress to recognize concurrent parent rights and student rights did not mean that federal lawmakers intended to prohibit university administrators from disclosing information to parents. However, like the clear distinction of age of majority, FERPA does not recognize a transition period between pre-adult and adult age groups. Because FERPA grants rights to either the parent or the student but not to both, the access rights of parents terminate when the student becomes a legal adult or enrolls in postsecondary courses.

Recent litigation indicates that some state laws vary in fundamental ways from federal education laws (Baker, 2001). The best advice for practitioners is to obtain clear direction from their legal counsel regarding state law standards and their relationship to federal FERPA rules.

Fortunately, legislators in some states intentionally designed student privacy laws to defer to the federal rules that govern education records (Baker, 2001). By deferring to federal law, state lawmakers thereby allow student affairs administrators to conduct day-to-day business relying primarily on FERPA rules to guide them.

The Broad Scope of FERPA Privacy Rights

FERPA protects the student's ability to access his or her education record information and control the disclosure of personally identifiable information. Senator James Buckley's original bill defined "education records" very broadly. Despite several minor amendments passed during the intervening years, the scope of FERPA remains broad today. Exceptions in the law limit a student's right to access financial aid information and medical records on file in the health center or counseling center. But practically all other records related to a student are subject to FERPA's access and disclosure provisions. For example, e-mail messages sent to the dean or notes from phone conversations with the student's parents must be disclosed to the student upon request if the messages have not yet been destroyed.

At the postsecondary level, parents have neither access rights nor disclosure rights. Once a student is admitted to the university and enrolls, the parent does not have the right to access the student's education records even if the student is financially dependent on the parent. In those cases where permission is required before university officials can disclose college education record information, the student—not the parent—decides whether the information will be disclosed to others. Because FERPA applies to all educational institutions that receive federal funds, private as well as public universities are obliged to observe FERPA or risk the loss of all federal loan money, research funds, and other grants.

In 1998, Congress amended FERPA to facilitate the disclosure of disciplinary information to parents of students under the age of twenty-one following an alcohol or illegal drug violation. The amendment does not define the disciplinary information as public information; however, if state laws permits disclosure, university officials may inform parents about the alcohol or drug infraction.

Observers who commented on the 1998 amendments to FERPA noted the increasingly prominent role of parents on college campuses (Weeks, 2001). Although some viewed the 1998 changes as indicative of a trend toward diminished student privacy rights, DE perceived the amendments quite differently (U.S. Department of Education, 2000). Federal officials saw the amendments as merely minor adjustments that did not radically alter the fundamental structure of the 1974 statute. While parents may be receiving more information as a result of the 1998 amendments, the new law did not grant to parents a right to force university administrators to disclose to them student record information without a court subpoena.

In essence, FERPA recognizes certain parent interests without creating parent rights enforceable in court. The interests of college student parents are protected in a number of ways under the statute. FERPA specifies that a student does not have the right to access financial aid information furnished to the university by the parents. In order to prohibit solicitors from contacting parents, moreover, university officials have the discretion to define home address and parent names as "nondirectory" information.

FERPA operates for the most part to protect families from social stigma associated with negative publicity. Where the student and the parents both want to avoid unwanted public scrutiny, FERPA's general prohibition on disclosing identifiable personal student information indirectly protects the privacy of the parents. Grades and disciplinary information, for example, cannot be disclosed without the student's express request. Therefore, low grades and disciplinary violations that might defame or embarrass the student's parents remain confidential.

FERPA Grounds for Disclosing Information to Parents

University administrators who choose to share information with parents cite one of several different FERPA provisions that allow for sharing information and disclosure. First, administrators are not prohibited from providing general information about college policy or practices. Second, disclosure is permitted once the student gives permission. Third, so long as state law does not prohibit disclosure, FERPA provides that student record information may be released to parents of students who are financially dependent on the parents. The financial dependence exception permits disclosure of all types of student record information—class attendance records as well as health emergencies, for instance. Fourth, administrators may disclose certain types of information without the student's permission, such as a health or safety emergency in which the parents need to know the information in order to assist the student. Finally, for those students not yet twenty-one years old, routine alcohol violations and drug violations may be shared with parents so long as state law does not prohibit disclosure.

Process Considerations. A campuswide policy of disclosing student record information to parents requires considerable administrative planning and record keeping. Logistical considerations complicate the task of designing a campus parental notice policy. Campus planners should bear in mind the following factors when considering a parental notification protocol:

- DE policy prohibits institutions from asking students to waive their FERPA rights as a condition for enrollment.
- Once a waiver form is signed consenting to disclosure, the student cannot be precluded from revoking his or her consent.
- A student accused of violating campus rules cannot be pressured to waive his or her FERPA rights as a condition for continued enrollment.
- The parent's payment of tuition or other university expenses does not automatically trigger the financial dependency provision of FERPA.
- DE defines financial dependency by referencing the IRS tax code regulations.
- Before disclosing information to parents under the tax dependency exception, some form of written record is required to verify the student's dependent status.
- A copy of the parent's tax return verifies a student's financial dependency only until the next year's tax return is due.

General Information Disclosure. Before considering management strategies for employing the student privacy exceptions, practitioners should keep in mind that FERPA rules implicitly allow administrators to answer basic parent questions without obtaining the student's written permission and without invoking a disclosure provision, so long as personally identifiable information is not disclosed. Because FERPA protects identifiable personal information only, administrators have the discretion to explain policies to any member of the public, including parents. Thus, when a parent inquires as to whether a notation will appear on the child's transcript regarding a nonacademic disciplinary sanction, the question can be answered in many cases by simply explaining the university's standard practice. Under this same approach, staff can explain the sanction policy for alcohol violations or outline the hearing process to an inquiring parent, for instance, without violating FERPA.

Because FERPA permits the release of directory information to any member of the public, some specific questions from parents can be answered readily without the student signing a release form. For example, if a parent inquires about the child's enrollment status, local address, or major field of study, university officials may disclose the answer as if they were responding to an inquiry from the public, so long as the particular category is listed in the annual FERPA notice as directory information and the student has not restricted its release. Thus, when a student is no longer enrolled and the parent wants to confirm the student's enrollment status, this fact can be disclosed even if the details of the student's circumstances may not be verifiable without written permission from the student. Similarly, when the parents of a crime victim inquire about the sanctions imposed upon the student assailant, information may be disclosed in some states by citing the FERPA rule that authorizes the release of "crime of violence" disciplinary sanction information to any member of the public.

Disclosure by Student Consent. Some institutions ask students to sign an information release form (also known as a "waiver") authorizing disclosure of FERPA-protected information to their parents. Other campuses require a student waiver as a prerequisite to mailing home the university bill. With the advent of online technology, some universities have abandoned the waiver strategy and instead created Internet "guest accounts" that parents can access using a password provided by the student.

Some campuses that rely on consent forms gear their consent process to twenty-first-century technology. With Internet tools widely available today, the DE accepts consent messages sent by students electronically in lieu of traditional signatures. Although collecting and tracking hard copy blanket waiver forms in the twentieth century posed significant logistical challenges, relying on blanket waiver forms in the twenty-first century may become the primary means for disclosing student record information to parents on many campuses. It is not illegal to present blanket disclosure forms to new students so long as institutions do not insist that students waive their FERPA rights as a condition for enrollment.

There are two major drawbacks to consent forms for disclosure to parents: the student's right to refuse consent and the student's right to revoke consent. Even when the student has signed a consent form at orientation, officials cannot continue to disclose student record information to the parents once the student revokes consent, unless there is an institutional record of the student's financial dependence on the parent. To verify the student's decision to revoke consent, university officials do not violate FERPA if they insist on a signed revocation statement rather than accepting a student's oral statement.

The university bill (U-bill) is one means for leveraging students and facilitating the disclosure of education record information to the parents. FERPA permits the registrar to send home the U-bill at the request of the student, but does not mandate it. Consequently, some institutions choose not to mail home the U-bill unless the student signs a statement agreeing

NEW DIRECTIONS FOR STUDENT SERVICES • DOI: 10.1002/ss

that the registrar will send the grade reports home at the end of the semester along with the U-bill. If the student refuses to sign the form authorizing release of the grade reports, the student is told that the U-bill will not be sent home without a signature on the release.

Internet access may create more direct—and more efficient—opportunities to facilitate the transmission of semester grades to the parents. On campuses where students can access their grades online from anywhere in the world, parents with Internet access at home can simply ask the student to print out on the home computer a copy of the student's grade report to share with the parents. So long as parents who are paying U-bills exercise their considerable leverage when negotiating with their students, the practice of printing out grades at home and accessing online guest accounts (as discussed earlier) may alleviate much of the administrative resources that would otherwise be spent transmitting academic record information to parents.

Disclosure Through the Financial Dependency Exception. The first question for any campus policy committee is whether or not to utilize the financial dependency exception as a general practice in communicating with parents. The answer will profoundly affect the means by which parent disclosure is facilitated on your campus.

FERPA regulation §99.31(a)(8) allows disclosure to parents without the student's prior written authorization if the student is "dependent" on the parents as defined by the Internal Revenue Code. Once financial dependency is established, administrators may disclose to parents any and all of the student's education record information regardless of the student's age and degree program. Undergraduate, graduate, and professional degree programs may use the financial dependency exception.

To verify financial dependency, universities need not require parents to show proof of actual financial support. In 1993, the DE Family Policy Compliance Office Director wrote, "this Office would support a policy of documenting a student's dependency status by requiring . . . a copy of the parent's most recent Federal income tax form [with the student listed as a dependent]." Alternatively, students could be required to identify their status as financially dependent or independent at the time of registration so long as (1) the students were advised in writing of the reason for the inquiry and (2) they were told of the FERPA consequences if they identified themselves as tax dependents (U.S. Department of Education, Rooker to Bienstock, 1993).

Thus, a tax return is not required if a student confirms in writing that his or her parents claimed him or her as a dependent for federal tax purposes. DE officials in 1998 suggested that every first-year student could be asked in writing at orientation whether the student's name appears on the parent's tax return as a dependent (Lowery, 2005). For those students who answer the question in writing in the affirmative, DE officials consider the confirmation just as reliable as a copy of the parent's tax return. The university must have some record as proof, however—either the most recent tax return or the student's admission of dependency.

DE correspondence clarifies what officials can do when a student self-identifies as nondependent, but the parent submits a copy of the most recent tax return showing the student as a dependent. According to the DE, the university may choose to invoke FERPA's tax-dependency exception and disclose information to the parent even though the student denied tax dependency status (U.S. Department of Education, Rooker to Bienstock, 1993).

One recent pronouncement by the DE Family Policy Compliance Office Director reaffirmed his office's expectation that some sort of written record be obtained before disclosing education record information to parents under the tax dependency exception. The director suggested that written confirmation from the student of dependency for federal tax purposes was unnecessary, as long as the student acknowledged the opportunity to refute the presumption of tax-dependent status. In answer to a question posed by the Association for Student Judicial Affairs, Lee Rooker wrote:

> Nothing in FERPA would preclude a university or college from advising each student during the registration process that their records will be disclosed to their parents upon request unless the parents do not claim that student as a dependent for income tax purposes. Students should be asked to indicate if they are claimed as a dependent and to *sign an acknowledgement* that they were provided the opportunity to notify the school that they are not dependents for income tax purposes. . . . In this way, the burden on a university of obtaining proof of a student's dependent status from a parent would be removed in most instances and colleges and universities could more readily distinguish those students who are dependent students from those who are not [Association for Student Judicial Affairs, 2007; emphasis added].

Although the DE has deliberately set out to minimize the need for collecting tax forms, there is still a requirement to maintain a record of the student's response, either to the question "Did your parents claim you as a dependent for federal tax purposes?" or to the question "Do you acknowledge you were provided the opportunity to notify the university that you are not dependent for income tax purposes?" Because parents file tax returns annually and dependency can change, the DE expects the university will check every year to confirm that a dependent student is still dependent for tax purposes (Lowery, 2005). Thus, if state law permits your institution to use the financial dependency exception, and your institution chooses to adopt this approach, campus administrators must keep up-to-date records of every dependent student's status as the student progresses toward graduation. Allowing students to record their responses electronically in lieu of hard copy release forms may help to minimize some of the paperwork burden on institutions.

Given the DE's paperwork expectations, this exception may not be pragmatic to operate on every campus. Lowery (2005) noted that small, private, residential colleges with traditional-age students are more inclined to rely on the dependency exception as the foundation of their parental notice policy. Because graduate students and nontraditional-age students are often self-supporting, the financial dependency exception may be more difficult to administer at public research universities.

Fortunately, FERPA rules simplify the disclosure process for those families with biological parents that file separate tax returns or reside in different locations. The term "parent" includes individuals acting as parents as well as biological parents. FERPA rules also simplify the process of communication in one other respect. An institution need not warn parents about the standard DE rule against redisclosure if the parents receive student record information under the tax dependency exception (U.S. Department of Education, Final Rule, 2000). In other words, FERPA does not prohibit the parent of a dependent student from sharing the student record information with a spouse, partner, relative, or anyone else. While the student could conceivably be embarrassed by public disclosure of academic or nonacademic information, DE is apparently convinced that parents of dependent students are not likely to circulate the education record information to a broad audience.

Disclosure of Alcohol and Other Drug Offenses. So long as state law permits such disclosure, administrators may use the alcohol and drug violation exception in lieu of collecting tax records or consent forms. When approved by Congress in 1998, this exception had immediate repercussions for parent notice practices on many campuses (Lowery, Palmer, and Gehring, 2005). Although the 1998 amendment is limited to alcohol and drug violations, it does cover all students under twenty-one years of age and it does permit disclosure of disciplinary information to parents with or without permission from the student. As with the financial dependency exception, use of the alcohol and drug provision is discretionary and not mandatory. For example, institutional policy designers can choose to notify parents after a second alcohol violation, but not after the first violation. Administrators may design a notification policy that best reflects institutional goals and philosophies.

Concerns about students' health and well-being motivated members of Congress to sponsor the 1998 amendment (Lowery, 2005). When a student self-reports an alcohol or drug violation to his or her parents, the 1998 amendment essentially expedites the process for verifying the accuracy of the disciplinary information the parents receive from the student. Rather than minimize the rights of students, the bill's sponsors intended to motivate parents to become more involved in intervening in instances of alcohol and drug use. Congress recognized that some young adults who died from alcohol-related injuries in the 1990s had not informed their parents after college officials had confronted their alcohol use through the judicial process.

The scope of the alcohol and drug exception was defined by the final FERPA regulations published in 2000. The DE rules permit disclosure to a parent of a postsecondary student under twenty-one "regarding the student's violation of any Federal, State, or local law, or of any rule or policy of the institution, governing the use or possession of alcohol or a controlled substance *if* the institution determines that the student has committed a disciplinary violation with respect to that use or possession" (U.S. Department of Education, Final Rule, 2000; emphasis added). Because the 1998 statute specifically noted that FERPA did not override state laws that prohibit universities from disclosing such information, administrators in California and other states with privacy laws broader than FERPA must look to local rules to determine whether they may utilize the alcohol and drug violation exception. As of 2006, the 2000 rules remained in effect without further amendment.

The language in the 1998 amendment may have seemed straightforward to politicians in Washington. However, in practice, it presented administrators with a number of difficult questions regarding the application of the law:

• When a student is found guilty of vandalism under the influence of alcohol, for example, what information can be disclosed to parents?
• Does the exception permit disclosure of alcohol-related crimes that take place off campus, if the conduct does not fall within the jurisdiction of the university's conduct rules?
• Must the institution's judicial process be exhausted—including the appeal stage—before disclosure is permitted?
• Are prescription drugs and tobacco considered "controlled substances" within the scope of the exception?
• When a notice letter is sent to parents, must the student receive a copy?
• What is the policy when students are caught with alcohol on the eve of their twenty-first birthday?

Fortunately, the DE's response did resolve several of these thorny issues. Based on the 2000 Final Rule, the policy appears to cover alcohol use, alcohol possession, intoxication, prescription drug violations, and illegal drug use and possession. The 1998 amendment does not cover cases where the student is currently twenty-one years old or where university rules do not prohibit the misconduct. Nor does the 1998 amendment permit disclosure in the case of tobacco possession or when a student is merely in the presence of drugs or alcohol without proof of use or possession of drugs or alcohol. When a notice letter is sent to parents, FERPA does not obligate officials to copy the students, ruled the DE, as long as a copy of the notice letter is maintained in the student's file.

Since the 1998 regulations cover "use" as well as "possession" violations, intoxication is a lawful event triggering parent disclosure so long as campus rules prohibit intoxication and the student is "determined" to be responsible or guilty. Thus, parents can be notified when students violate a rule under the influence of alcohol even if campus rules prohibiting use and possession of alcohol were not violated.

Because the DE declined to define the terms "determination" and "disciplinary violation," local administrators have considerable discretion when applying the federal law to the particular circumstances of their campus. In a vandalism and excessive noise case, for instance, nothing in the DE rules explicitly prohibits administrators from informing parents about the vandalized dormitory property or about the noise violation if the student was also found in possession of alcohol.

The 2000 DE rules do make clear that "presence" violations are not triggering events. Thus, when a student is present in another resident's dormitory room where alcohol is found and the student did not consume or possess the alcohol, disclosure to parents without the consent of the student is not permissible under the 1998 amendment, even if campus rules prohibit being in the presence of alcohol.

The age of the student may also preclude parental notification in those cases where the individual caught with alcohol or drugs is only a few days short of his or her twenty-first birthday. Because the statute applies only to students under twenty-one years of age, the DE determined that disclosure is not permitted under this exception once a student reaches the age of twenty-one, regardless of when the violation occurred. Thus, even if the violation occurred before the student's birthday, the process must conclude before the student turns twenty-one in order for administrators to disclose the violation without the student's permission.

Off-campus violations can be disclosed to parents as long as institutional rules extend beyond the boundaries of campus and alcohol or other drugs are involved. Notice is prohibited for off-campus violations that do not fall under the campus alcohol and drug rules. Off-campus violations do not automatically trigger the exception, because a student must be determined to have violated institutional disciplinary rules in order for parents to be notified.

For campuses that operate "substance-free" policies, tobacco violations do not appear to fall within the scope of the 1998 amendment. Thus, parents can be notified when a student is caught smoking marijuana, but not when an underage student is smoking cigarettes. The 2000 DE rules apparently do cover prescription drug violations, because the term "controlled substance" is used interchangeably in the DE's commentary with the word "drug."

In terms of the timing of the notice to parents, disclosure can be made as soon as the violation is "determined" according to local rules. One might have predicted that the DE would recognize a hearing as an essential component of the determination process, but the DE explicitly refused to do so. Thus, even though hearings are common components of campus judicial procedures, the 2000 regulations do not contain any procedural prerequisites to disclosure.

In practice, the exhaustion of the hearing process or the appeals process is the event that commonly triggers notice to parents. Lowery found that "most institutions with a policy or practice of parental notification typically make the notification only after the conclusion of the disciplinary proceeding" (2005, p. 46).

That the DE provides few barriers to notifying parents following alcohol and drug disciplinary infractions creates a number of administrative policy questions for campus policy designers. Logistical considerations rather than legal considerations may impose greater challenges to practitioners assigned to implement parent notice policies based on the 1998 amendments. Lowery, Palmer, and Gehring (2005) found that high administrative costs have discouraged some campuses from notifying parents in writing about every instance of an alcohol or drug infraction. Educational philosophy may also influence campus policy designers to decline the practice of contacting parents. For those who find that disclosure does not facilitate healthy parent-student communication and impedes the maturation process for the student, the possibility of notifying parents in nonemergency situations may be rejected. In the worst cases, notice invites parents to disrupt the disciplinary process in a manner that is counterproductive to the educational process (Lowery, Palmer, and Gehring, 2005).

The administrative cost of notifying parents depends, of course, on the number of alcohol and drug violations and the means of communication (whether telephone, U.S. mail, or electronic mail). In 2001 the Inter-Association Task Force on Alcohol and Other Substance Abuse Issues (2001) warned that "the amount of time necessary to successfully implement" an aggressive parental notification plan "is extensive." "Regardless if you use letters, phone calls, or a combination, a good deal of staff energies will be spent in not only the initial contact but handling parent phone calls seeking additional information or the desire to provide their own input," concluded the 2001 Task Force. If parents "go up the chain of command," senior administrators will receive more calls from parents.

Despite the logistical burdens and educational conundrums posed by parent notice, many institutions implemented parental notification policies for alcohol and other drug violations within a few years following its passage (Lowery, Palmer, and Gehring, 2005). Patterns and practices varied, however, by region, by type of institution (small or large, private or public), and by the extent to which officials deemed alcohol abuse a serious campus problem.

In order to minimize administrative costs, some institutions in the late 1990s relied on form letters in lieu of original letters. Form letters to parents might communicate basic information such as the date and location of the infraction but ignore the details of the case, such as the amount of alcohol discovered (Brooks, 1999). Some institutions notified parents after every violation (Lowery, Palmer, and Gehring, 2005), and on other campuses a second violation triggered the first letter home. Residential status provides another means to tailor the parental notice system to maximize educational effectiveness. At the University of Iowa, where first-year students filled 70 percent of residence hall space in 2006, parents of residential students received notice of routine alcohol and drug infractions, but parents of off-campus residents did not.

In short, the 1998 amendments created new means to facilitate notice to parents, opportunities that many campuses utilized. But notifying parents of alcohol and drug violations does take a toll on institutional resources. It remains to be seen whether the costs are so substantial as to outweigh the educational advantage for the student. The alcohol and drug exception also raised new questions about state privacy laws and the interrelationship between state and federal laws. Because state law controls the disclosure of disciplinary information to parents under this FERPA exception, administrators would be well advised to seek legal advice about parent disclosure rules in their jurisdiction and the extent to which parents have the right to force disclosure. Fortunately, the question of parent access under federal law is well settled.

Parent Interests Under Federal Law

For those institutions that choose to disclose student record information to parents, FERPA does not require that both parents be notified if one parent is notified, nor does it require that parents be notified of every development on campus. Thus, a missed class or a minor disciplinary infraction, for instance, need not be reported to parents just because parents get called about alcohol and drug violations. This is true even if parents have submitted a copy of their latest tax return or an information release form has been signed by the student. In fact, parents of dependent students do not have an enforceable right under federal law to receive any student record information, even semester grade reports or U-bills.

The question of a parent's ability to force disclosure has been the subject of speculation for some time. Weeks (1985), citing the comments of FERPA sponsor James Buckley, predicted that parents would some day go to court to force institutions to disclose information under the financial dependency exception. To date, no court has so ruled, however. Because judges ordinarily are reluctant to disregard the letter of the statute, which clearly vests upon the student all FERPA rights in controlling his or her postsecondary records, the comments of the law's sponsor may carry little legal weight in the event a suit is filed by a parent who paid the student's tuition but was denied access to the student's grade reports.

DE officials are even less likely than the courts to satisfy a parent's expectation of notification. While the parent is entitled to file a formal complaint with the DE in lieu of a lawsuit, such a complaint would likely result in a denial of relief. When explaining FERPA disclosure provisions, DE officials have consistently stuck to the plain language of the statute. In a 2000 statement published in the *Federal Register*, the DE noted that once a tax return is received, the institution has "the discretion to, although it need not, disclose the student's education records to the parent of the student" (U.S. Department of Education, Final Rule, 2000). Similarly, a Frequently Asked Question web site maintained by the DE provides the following explanation:

> Q5: If I am a parent of a college student, do I have the right to see my child's education records, especially if I pay the bill?

A: The rights under FERPA transfer from the parents to the student, once the student turns eighteen years old or enters a postsecondary institution at any age. However, although the rights under FERPA have now transferred to the student, a school may disclose information . . . to the parents of the student, without the student's consent, if the student is a dependent for tax purposes. Neither the age of the student nor the parent's status as a custodial parent is relevant. If a student is claimed as a dependent by either parent for tax purposes, then either parent may have access under this provision [U.S. Department of Education, "Frequently Asked Questions," 2007].

When faced with parental pressure to disclose information, some staff members may respond by complying with the request immediately without first obtaining the parent's tax return. Such a pattern of administrative practice, when applied on a large scale to all students, entails certain legal risks. The DE has a practice of investigating alleged FERPA violations when a student files a formal complaint with the DE. Although no university has yet been stripped of federal funding as a result of a FERPA violation, DE finding letters usually include a threat to cut off federal funds in the event the prohibited practice is not immediately stopped.

The risk of liability will certainly increase if Congress amends FERPA to create a private right of student action. Following the U.S. Supreme Court's ruling in *Gonzaga University* v. *Doe* (2002), one member of Congress sponsored a bill to amend FERPA and create a private right of action to enforce FERPA in court. Although the right-to-sue bill did not get out of committee in 2003, a similar measure could be reintroduced in the near future (Lowery, 2007).

Suicidal Behavior and the Legal Consequences of Nondisclosure

Few situations on campus are more difficult than staff members' knowledge that a student has deliberately swallowed a large quantity of pills, cut through the skin with a knife, or threatened to commit suicide. The question of disclosing suicidal behavior to the parents is not merely a matter of interpreting FERPA. Because wrongful death allegations made by the parents may include a failure-to-notify claim, student affairs practitioners must keep in mind the possibility that state common law or statutory law may require notification in some situations. Practitioners are advised to work closely with institutional legal counsel when designing the campus suicide prevention policy and drafting individual letters in the aftermath of self-destructive behavior.

Much of the legal risk arises when a student who attempts suicide on campus later completes a suicide. The past several years have witnessed a remarkable number of failure-to-notify lawsuits filed by parents of students who committed suicide on campus (Baker, 2005). Both private and public universities have been sued when the family learned afterward of a previous suicide attempt on campus. The suits have been filed in different states, some in federal court and others in state court, and different causes of action have been brought. At least one failure-to-notify claim was grounded on a breach-of-contract theory, while in *Jain* v. *State of Iowa* (2000) the family based their argument on FERPA. The Iowa Supreme Court ultimately rejected the argument that FERPA mandates notification. However, in suits filed under a wrongful death theory, some courts have been willing to permit the jury to explore whether a special legal relationship existed once staff became aware of the student's history of suicidal behavior (Pavela, 2006). Because a college student's death represents a tremendous loss of youth and potential, jurors may be especially sympathetic to the family's loss.

When the dean learns of a suicide attempt and elects to disclose the details of the suicide attempt to the student's parents, the dean need look no further than the health and safety emergency exception in FERPA to justify the breach of confidentiality (Family Educational Rights and Privacy Act, 34 C.F.R. §99.36(a), 2006). The emergency exception applies to situations where nonschool personnel need to know information in order to protect the health or safety of the student or other individuals. Parents of college students are included within the scope of the emergency exception, and recent action by the DE confirmed this fact. Two months following the Virginia Tech tragedy, the DE's Web site specified that FERPA permits institutional officials to "disclose information from education records to parents if a health or safety emergency involves their son or daughter" (U.S. Department of Education, 2007). On March 24, 2008, the DE proposed to revise section 99.36(a) to include "parents of an eligible student" within the category of "appropriate parties" who can be contacted by school officials when necessary to protect the health or safety of the student (U.S. Department of Education, Family Policy Compliance Office, 2008, p. 15601).

So that school officials are not discouraged from utilizing the health and safety exception, the DE removed language on March 24, 2008 from the original rule that warned officials that the DE would "strictly construe" the school's decision to invoke the health and safety exception. In its place, the DE's proposed rule explains that when the health or safety threat is "articulable and significant," information may be disclosed to persons whose knowledge of the information is necessary to protect the student or other individuals. When interpreting the meaning of "articulable and significant threats," the DE intends to defer to the judgment of school officials, according to the new rule. "If, based on the information available at the time of the determination, there is a rational basis for the determination, the Department will not substitute its judgment for that of the educational agency or institution in evaluating the circumstances and making its determination" (U.S. Department of Education, Family Policy Compliance Office, 2008, p. 15601).

Although college officials must still meet the "articulable and significant" standard to invoke the health and safety exception, past DE practice strongly indicates that federal officials will not question the use of the health and safety exception to disclose information to parents of a suicidal college student. Over a thirty-year period, in not a single instance did the DE officially reprimand a university for contacting parents following a suicide attempt without the student's permission (Baker, 2005). With regard to behavior less severe than a suicide attempt, a number of consultants believe the health and safety exception covers many forms of disturbing conduct. Two higher education attorneys recently concluded that "Safety concerns warranting disclosure could include a student's suicidal statements or ideations, unusually erratic and angry behaviors, or similar conduct that others would reasonably see as posing a risk of serious harm" (Tribbensee and McDonald, 2007).

The FERPA exception does not, however, permit physicians or therapists to disclose medical record information to parents. Medical records laws allow physicians and therapists to contact parents under certain circumstances, but these hospital laws are separate and distinct from FERPA (Rowe, 2005). Depending on the scope of the medical record disclosure provisions, doctors and therapists who treat a suicidal student may or may not have legal authority to inform the parents or the dean about the suicide attempt.

Because exceptions in medical records law for emergency situations do not exactly parallel the exceptions in student education records laws, it may be advisable for campus planners to operate a dual system for notifying family members (Baker, 2005). Under a dual-system arrangement, the dean of students or some other nonmedical staff member is assigned to contact parents following a campus suicide attempt, regardless of whether physicians or therapists are doing the same.

If campus planners decide to invoke the FERPA emergency exception as part of the suicide prevention plan, the following practical questions must be addressed:

- Which student affairs staff member is in the best position to collect relevant documents and contact the parents?
- Since the process for gathering relevant documents may take some time, how long does the designated contact person wait before notifying the parents?
- By what means do you contact the parents (telephone, U.S. Mail, electronic mail, or in person)?
- Who is considered a parent, and which parent gets the call if the parents are not living in the same household?
- Under what circumstances is disclosure not undertaken? For instance, are parents contacted if there is a history of family sexual abuse that affected the student's mental health and contributed to the suicide attempt?

• What information is included in the letter? For example, should you attach a copy of the suicide note?

The recent spurt in campus suicide litigation underscores the importance of contacting the parents in writing even if they have already received a telephone call. Once notified, parents typically do not intervene to persuade the suicidal student to withdraw (Baker, 2006). Because the family may not understand the risk inherent in remaining enrolled, it is important that parents receive the salient details of the suicide attempt and know that campus officials do not monitor students after they leave the hospital. In explaining to parents the campus resources available to suicidal students, university officials would be well advised to mention the possibility of a subsequent episode of self-destructive behavior. The sample emergency letters printed in Appendix B illustrate how one campus explains the university's inability to monitor the student.

In court, failure-to-notify claims tend to be filed as a secondary cause of action to a claim of medical malpractice or a claim of wrongful death. To date, no American court has upheld a failure-to-notify claim filed by parents of college students. The fact that K–12 officials in some states have an affirmative duty to notify parents following suicidal behavior on school grounds does suggest the litigation pattern may change. For college students not yet eighteen years of age, officials may be required to notify parents of suicidal behavior even if state law does not require notice to parents of students eighteen years or older. To date, no court has issued a ruling on the notice requirements following suicidal behavior by a minor student attending college.

Over time, courts in some states may treat the postsecondary campus similarly to the K–12 campus. A good barometer for future legal developments may be the evolution of the "special relationship" doctrine in tort law, which in some states could be applied to nonmedical staff who are aware that a college student living on campus is suicidal.

The definition of a "health or safety emergency" may also evolve in the near future. Following violent incidents on college campuses in 2007, several members of Congress sponsored a bill to clarify that university officials may legally contact parents following an attempted suicide or some other event that posed a "significant risk" to the student's health. Unfortunately, the unintended consequence of this bill, if it becomes law, may be to discourage calls to the parents in cases where the perceived risk is not obviously at the level of a "significant risk."

Working with Parents of Students Not Yet Eighteen Years Old

Communicating with parents of minors attending college may become a significant responsibility for student affairs staff as the twenty-first century progresses. As more high schools accept college courses for high school credit, and as more programs for talented and gifted young students take root, university campuses may see an increasing percentage of students not yet eighteen years of age.

Fortunately, FERPA very clearly defines the educational records privacy rights due to university students under eighteen years of age: they enjoy the same rights as adult students. This means that even high school students who are taking college courses on a part-time basis are entitled to the same FERPA rights and protections afforded to high school graduates attending college. The principle of universality does not apply, however, in other areas of family law. Because state laws governing contract rights, medical treatment, and tort law treat seventeen-year-olds as minors even if they are high school graduates, university officials may find themselves advising parents of minor students differently from parents of adult students. In order to explain how campus policies apply to minor students, sending a standard letter to parents of students who will turn eighteen years of age sometime after they arrive on campus may be sound practice. The letter might explain, for instance, that routine medical care cannot be provided to minors without the parent's permission.

Writing to parents of minors may prove especially useful with regard to student purchases on credit and other business transactions. In those states where contracts cannot be enforced in court for students under eighteen years of age, campus protocol may preclude seventeen-year-olds from charging meals and books on the university ID card. To facilitate use of the charge card, cashiers and treasurers on some campuses offer a form for parents to sign agreeing to reimburse the institution for any and all charges made by the minor student. The sample letter in Appendix B shows one approach to this problem.

Furthermore, the letter to parents of minor students might clarify residence hall policy. If minors are not segregated by age and are not treated any differently from adult residents with regard to supervision, explaining this policy to the parents in writing may ensure against miscommunication while avoiding potential legal questions if the minor student is injured after engaging in high-risk behavior. Because campus residence halls are designed for adults who do not require institutional supervision, parents may wish to consider alternate housing arrangements for those minor students who are not yet mature enough to live independently. For fifteen- and sixteen-year-old students who are not old enough to consent to sexual intercourse under state law, it may be critical to convey residence hall policy information to their parents prior to students' arrival on campus.

Implications

In defining the scope of college student privacy rights through FERPA in 1974, Congress neither mandated nor prohibited disclosure to parents in every instance. This principle remains true today. As long as university officials use one of the privacy rule exceptions in FERPA and comply with state law when disclosing information to parents, the student does not have a legal basis to challenge the university's disclosure practice. The college student may complain to the DE's Office of Family Compliance or file a lawsuit, but neither the DE nor a judge is likely to rule against the university's practice as long as the disclosure falls under one of the privacy law exceptions. Conversely, a complaint filed by a parent who did not receive student record information from the university is likely to be rejected.

Select Disclosure Options Carefully. In developing a parent notice policy, the proper question for campus planners is not whether parents can be notified but what type of information should be disclosed to the parents and how. Each parent disclosure exception in FERPA has its own educational implications as well as paperwork demands. Of the several disclosure exceptions in FERPA, no single exception is ideally suited for every campus. If student information on file across the campus is not centralized in one office, the process of designing a practical plan for disclosing information to parents will not be easy.

Even on campuses that centralize student record information, institutional planners would be well advised to compare and contrast the advantages and disadvantages of each disclosure option when selecting the primary means for facilitating parent notice consistent with FERPA and state law. For those campus planners who are particularly concerned about first-year students, two different plans may be developed, one designed to facilitate regular communication with parents of students recently graduated from high school and a second plan designed for parents of upper-class students who are contacted only in emergency situations without permission from the student. No matter what plan is adopted, student affairs staff should always remember that FERPA regulates only identifiable personal information. When the dean's office is called, the parent's concerns can be addressed in many situations by simply stating institutional policy. The ability to explain general policy may allay the parent's concerns as long as the parent does not request a copy of the incident report.

In this age of Internet and cell phone communication, some campus officials deliberately encourage parents to communicate directly with the students on a regular basis about the student's academic progress. Printing the grade report at home or sharing the computer password with the parents often facilitates verification of semester grades and other basic information without the need for administrative intervention (although sharing passwords creates another issue not covered in this volume). Such a plan may be preferable, given the logistical burdens imposed by federal law. As FERPA is currently interpreted, the financial dependency exception requires assertive administration action to obtain the parent's most recent tax return or generate records of student responses to questions about their parents' tax return. Asking every student to sign a blank information release form at the time of enrollment may avoid some of the administrative burdens presented by the tax dependency exception. But disclosure to parents is not permitted for those students who decline to sign the consent form or later revoke the release.

In short, there are a number of practical ways within FERPA to ensure that semester grades and other basic record information are made available to parents. If Congress continues to carve out exceptions to FERPA in order to facilitate disclosure to parents following certain high-risk situations, campus planners may prefer a multifaceted plan. In 2006, campus officials could decline to collect tax returns and consent forms and rely instead on other means to communicate with parents. Provided state law does not prevent such a strategy, one plan might consist of (1) posting on the Internet grades and class schedules accessible to the student and a guest designated by the student; (2) agreeing to send U-bills home to parents only after the student authorizes the release of semester grades along with the U-bill; (3) notifying parents in the event of a health emergency; (4) notifying parents of alcohol and drug violations; and (5) maintaining information release forms on file that are customized specifically for each office, as opposed to a blanket consent form that would cover all student record information on campus. Examples of customized forms include a medical release form in the student health center, an academic information release form in the academic advising center, and a residence hall disciplinary information release form for university housing staff.

Consider Technology Solutions for Disclosure Consent. Although FERPA was devised during the pre-Internet era, twenty-first-century technology can facilitate parent access to many varieties of education records without the need to obtain written permission from the student. By giving students online access to their grades, class schedule, and other academic information, parents who have an Internet connection at home can simply ask the student to access online information together. When the student is on campus, some administrative software enhancements allow students to provide parents with a "guest account," giving them access to the student's financial and academic record. Under the guest account arrangement, parents who have the student's electronic password can check the child's registration, U-bill, and semester grades, for instance. Electronic technology may also facilitate the disclosure of nonacademic information to parents in lieu of standard release forms. As long as the student is willing to grant permission and indicates his or her approval in an electronic message, DE regulations permit universities to accept electronic signatures from students (including facsimile signatures) without a hard copy signature (U.S. Department of Education, Final Rule, 2004).

Modern technology will not, however, facilitate parent access to information in every situation. Emergency situations often require that campus officials disclose identifiable personal information unilaterally to the parents. Disciplinary information, which is not ordinarily centralized in electronic files, may also be difficult to share with parents. Students, meanwhile, may refuse to provide electronic passwords to their parents. Because FERPA generally prohibits the unauthorized disclosure of student record information, campus planners must consider utilizing the financial dependency provision, collecting student signatures on consent forms, invoking the alcohol and drug violation exception, or employing a combination of these FERPA disclosure provisions. The disclosure policy adopted by your campus may be influenced by logistical considerations and student development philosophy, among other factors.

Keep Federal Laws, State Laws, and Campus Policies Close at Hand. To ensure that FERPA is observed, a student affairs professional would be well advised to keep several resources on hand for reference in resolving disclosure questions that arise from time to time. Because decisions to disclose or not disclose student record information are often handled on a case-by-case basis—without consulting with legal counsel in every instance—a copy of the latest FERPA regulations (*Code of Federal Regulations,* volume 34, part 99) should be at your fingertips. Guidance statements published by the Family Policy Compliance Office of the DE should be readily accessible. The DE's 2000 Final Rule contains especially relevant commentary on the parent notice exceptions passed in 1998.

Equally important are state law documents governing the rights of young adults. Where state privacy laws affect the administration of student records on your campus, relevant materials explaining applicable state law should be at your disposal. Consulting with your institutional attorney may be particularly beneficial with regard to the applicability of the 1998 FERPA amendments. Information release forms must be prepared by institutional attorneys with both state law and federal rules in mind. When drafting emergency notice letters to parents following suicide attempts—as well as any other events with potential legal implications—student affairs staff should consult with university legal counsel (Baker, 2005).

Watch Federal Legislation for Changes in Interpretation and Law. The reference materials will change, of course, as student privacy law continues to evolve. Kaplin and Lee (2006) note that the rights due students are in a state of flux. Because the constitutional principle of preemption forbids state lawmakers from undercutting the scope of federal privacy laws, one might predict that any additional changes in student privacy laws designed to facilitate disclosure to parents would take place at the federal level.

In Congress, a range of FERPA amendments have been proposed since 2000. Although none of the recent proposals had been enacted as of 2006, it is noteworthy that some legislators prefer to go on record as supporting both student rights and parental interests. The same lawmakers who proposed to empower students to file lawsuits in 2003 as a means to enforce their federal privacy rights were also prepared to mandate parent notice in situations where the student's health was in danger (Lowery, 2007). In the event that Congress once again changes FERPA, relevant state laws must be examined carefully in order to determine whether a change in state law is necessary before the new federal rules can be utilized.

Review Institutional Practices Regularly. As the debate in Congress continues, campus planners should periodically review the institution's annual FERPA policy statement and update it as necessary to ensure its relevance and reflect any changes in state law, federal law, and local practice. Summer orientation materials for new students and parents should be reviewed carefully to ensure that parental disclosure policies are clearly explained. Even on a campus where contacting parents is a common practice, institutional representatives should be wary of promising to notify parents of every new development. Internal policy statements should never refer to parents' interests in receiving student record information as parent "rights" (Baker, 2005).

Understanding FERPA and complying with the letter of the law is one important component of ethical decision making. Ultimately, the task of defining the educational purposes served by parental notice poses a much more challenging problem than interpreting federal and state privacy laws. Elsewhere in this publication, student affairs practitioners have identified situations where parental knowledge is likely to aid in the student's educational development.

Balance Student Privacy and Parental Influence. Balancing student privacy rights and the perceived benefits of parental notification may prove challenging for many institutions. Given the increase in parental involvement, parents will certainly push to obtain information to guide their student's success. However, as student affairs administrators we must continually keep the rights of students in the forefront of our policies. Student affairs officers who have the discretionary authority to disclose student record information to parents must also keep the student's educational interests foremost in mind when deciding whether or not to disclose.

References

Association for Student Judicial Affairs. *FERPA Questions for Lee Rooker, Director of the Family Policy Compliance Office, U.S. Department of Education.* Retrieved Oct. 26, 2007, from www.asjaonline.org/en/art/?328.

Baker, T. R. "State Preemption of Federal Law: The Strange Case of College Student Disciplinary Records Under FERPA." *Education Law Reporter,* 2001, *149,* 283–319.

Baker, T. R. "Notifying Parents Following a College Student Suicide Attempt: A Review of Case Law and FERPA, and Recommendations for Practice." *NASPA Journal,* 2005, *42,* 513–533. Retrieved Oct. 26, 2007, from http://publications.naspa.org/naspajournal/vol42/iss4/art7.

Baker, T. R. "Parents of Suicidal College Students: What Deans, Judges, and Legislators Should Know About Campus Research Findings." *NASPA Journal,* 2006, *43,* 164–181. Retrieved Oct. 26, 2007, from http://publications.naspa.org/naspajournal/vol43/iss4/art10.

Brooks, T. F. "The Pros and Cons of Notifying Parents of Disciplinary Action." Paper presented at the Association for Student Judicial Affairs International Conference, Clearwater Beach, Fla., Feb. 7, 1999.

Family Educational Rights and Privacy Act of 1974, 20 U.S.C. 1232g; 34 C.F.R. §99 (2006).

Gonzaga University v. *Doe*, 536 U.S. 273 (2002).

Inter-Association Task Force on Alcohol and Other Substance Abuse Issues. *Parent Notification.* 2001. Retrieved March 1, 2007, from www.iatf.org/parent1a.html.

Jain v. *State of Iowa*, 617 N.W.2d 293 (Iowa, 2000).

Kaplin, W. A., and Lee, B. A. *The Law of Higher Education: A Comprehensive Guide to Legal Implications of Administrative Decision Making.* (4th ed.) San Francisco: Jossey-Bass, 2006.

Lowery, J. W. "Legal Issues Regarding Partnering with Parents: Misunderstood Federal Laws and Potential Sources of Institutional Liability." In K. Keppler, R.H.Mullendore, and A. Carey (eds.), *Partnering with Parents of Today's College Students.* National Association of Student Personnel Administrators, 2005.

Lowery, J. W. "Engaging with Washington: A Legislative Update for Student Judicial Affairs." Paper presented at the Association for Student Judicial Affairs annual conference, Clearwater Beach, Fla., Feb. 9, 2007.

Lowery, J. W., Palmer, C. J., and Gehring, D. D. "Policies and Practices of Parental Notification for Student Alcohol Violations." *NASPA Journal,* 2005, *42,* 415–429. Retrieved March 1, 2007, from http://publications.naspa.org/naspajournal/vol42/iss4/art2.

Pavela, G. "Today's College Students Need Both Freedom and Structure." *Chronicle of Higher Education,* July 29, 1992.

Pavela, G. *Questions and Answers on College Student Suicide: A Law and Policy Perspective.* Asheville, N.C.: College Administrative Publications, 2006.

Rowe, L. P. "What Judicial Officers Need to Know About the HIPAA Privacy Rule." *NASPA Journal,* 2005, *42,* 498–512. Retrieved Aug. 6, 2007, from http://publications.naspa.org/naspajournal/vol42/iss4/art6.

Tribbensee, N. E., and McDonald, S. J. "FERPA and Campus Safety." *NACUANOTE,* 2007, *5*(4).

U.S. Department of Education, Family Policy Compliance Office. "Disclosure of Information from Education Records to Parents of Postsecondary Students." Retrieved July 2, 2007, from www.ed.gov/policy/gen/guid/fpco/hottopics/ht-parents-postsecstudents.html.

U.S. Department of Education, Family Policy Compliance Office. "Frequently Asked Questions." Retrieved May 1, 2007, from www.ed.gov/policy/gen/guid/fpco/faq.html.

U.S. Department of Education, Family Policy Compliance Office. LeRoy S. Rooker to Robert E. Bienstock, University of New Mexico (Oct. 29, 1993).

U.S. Department of Education, Family Policy Compliance Office. "Family Educational Rights and Privacy Act, Proposed Rule, 34 C.F.R. §99," 73 Federal Register 15573 (March 24, 2008).

U.S. Department of Education, Final Rule 34 C.F.R. Part 99. 65 *Federal Register* 41852 (July 6, 2000).

U.S. Department of Education, Final Rule 34 C.F.R. Part 99. 69 *Federal Register* 21669 (Apr. 21, 2004).

United States of America v. *The Miami University and The Ohio State University*, 294 F.3d 737 (6th Cir. 2002).

Weeks, K. M. "The Buckley Amendment and College Students' Parents: Limitations and Allowance." In R. D. Cohen (ed.), *Working with the Parents of College Students.* New Directions for Student Services, no. 32. San Francisco: Jossey-Bass, 1985.

Weeks, K. M. "Family-Friendly FERPA Policies: Affirming Parental Partnerships." In B. V. Daniel and B. R. Scott (eds.), *Consumers, Adversaries, and Partners: Working with Families of Undergraduates.* New Directions for Student Services, no. 94. San Francisco: Jossey-Bass, 2001.

THOMAS R. BAKER is associate dean of students at the University of Iowa.

New Directions for Student Services • DOI: 10.1002/ss

APPENDIX A: PARENT PROGRAM SURVEY

1. Please indicate your level of satisfaction with the college's or university's communications with parents and guardians of students.
___ Very satisfied
___ Satisfied
___ Dissatisfied
___ Very dissatisfied

2. How often do you typically communicate with your student?
___ More than once a day
___ Daily
___ Two or three times a week
___ About weekly
___ Two or three times a month
___ About once a month
___ Less than once a month

3. How do you *most often* communicate with your student?

	Very Frequently	Frequently	Less Frequently	Rarely	Never
In person	☐	☐	☐	☐	☐
Student's cell phone	☐	☐	☐	☐	☐
Student's landline phone	☐	☐	☐	☐	☐
E-mail	☐	☐	☐	☐	☐
Regular mail	☐	☐	☐	☐	☐
Instant messaging	☐	☐	☐	☐	☐

4. How often do you visit campus?
___ Rarely or not at all
___ Once or twice a semester
___ About once a month
___ More than once a month
___ More than once a week

5. The college or university sends an electronic newsletter to parents every two weeks, and a print newsletter is mailed to parents quarterly. Have you

---

The questions shown here are adapted from University of Minnesota's biannual parent survey.

NEW DIRECTIONS FOR STUDENT SERVICES, no. 122, Summer 2008 © Wiley Periodicals, Inc.
Published online in Wiley InterScience (www.interscience.wiley.com) • DOI: 10.1002/ss.278

discussed with your student any of the topics covered in either the e-mail or print newsletter?

___ Yes

___ No

If yes, please list any topics you recall discussing with your student:

_____

_____

6. Did you attend parent orientation when your student first enrolled at the college or university?

___ Yes

___ No

7. If you answered yes to the last question, what was the most useful? What was missing? If you answered no, why did you decide not to attend?

_____

_____

8. Please indicate whether you are aware of the following programs and services for parents.

Parent orientation	___ Yes	___ No
Homecoming or parent weekend events	___ Yes	___ No
Parent Program Web site	___ Yes	___ No
Parent e-mail listserv	___ Yes	___ No
Parent Program director to answer your questions	___ Yes	___ No

9. Please indicate your level of satisfaction with the college's or university's programs and services for parents and guardians of students.

___ Very satisfied

___ Satisfied

___ Dissatisfied

___ Very dissatisfied

10. What other services would you like to see for parents? _____

_____

_____

11. Please indicate your level of agreement with the following statement: "I feel that the (name of institution) includes parents in the college or university community."

___ Strongly agree

___ Agree

___ Disagree

___ Strongly disagree

12. What year is your student in now?
____ Freshman
____ Sophomore
____ Junior
____ Senior
____ Graduate student
____ Unsure

13. This year, what has been your greatest concern regarding your student?
____ Health and safety
____ Finances
____ Academics
____ Campus or community involvement opportunities
____ Career planning
____ Personal relationships
____ None
____ Other_____

14. This year, on what topic has your student most often requested assistance or advice from you?
____ Health and safety
____ Finances
____ Academics
____ Campus or community involvement opportunities
____ Career planning
____ Personal relationships
____ None
____ Other_____

15. Where does your student live?
____ At home
____ On campus
____ Sorority or fraternity
____ Apartment or house near campus (non-university housing)
____ Other

16. What is your student's gender?
____ Male
____ Female

17. Please indicate where you live.
____ Within xx miles of campus
____ Beyond xx miles, but within the state
____ Neighboring state [Specify state where most out-of-state students come from.]
____ Neighboring state [Specify additional states as needed.]
____ Other (please provide name of state or country)_____

18. What is your highest level of education?
___ Less than high school diploma
___ High school graduate
___ Associate degree
___ Bachelor's degree
___ Master's degree
___ Ph.D. or professional degree

19. If you attended college, how would you compare the level of your involvement and communication with your student to the involvement and communication your parents had with you during college?
___ Much more involved
___ More involved
___ About the same
___ Less involved
___ Much less involved
___ Not applicable

20. What is your relationship to your student?

___ Mother	___ Father
___ Grandmother	___ Grandfather
___ Aunt	___ Uncle
___ Foster mother	___ Foster father
___ Other	

21. How old are you? _____

APPENDIX B: SAMPLE PARENT LETTERS

Sample Health and Safety Letter for Suicide Attempt

March 4, 2008

Mr. and Mrs. X
101 Parent Drive
Some Town, USA 00000

Dear Mr. and Mrs. X:

Recently, I received information about your daughter, Student, who was transported to the University Hospitals & Clinics from her residence hall after an apparent suicide attempt. It is my understanding that hospital personnel telephoned you while Student was undergoing treatment. It was reported to me that you came to campus and visited your daughter shortly after she was released from the hospital and returned to her residence hall.

It is the policy of the Student Services Office to notify a student's parents in cases such as this where the student's health or safety appeared to be seriously threatened on campus as a result of self-destructive behavior. In order to ensure that you are aware of the full details of this serious situation, the facts known to the Office of the Vice President for Student Services are provided below.

[Insert details of the incident here.]

Recently, Student met with the residence hall coordinator and discussed the self-destructive behavior policy. Student acknowledged that she violated the policy. Because she put herself at risk by intentionally injuring herself, Student has been placed on disciplinary probation. If she were to violate university conduct rules on a subsequent occasion during the academic year, Student would more than likely be suspended from the university for a minimum of one semester. Student agreed to complete a counseling evaluation at the University Counseling Center as soon as possible.

I am concerned about Student's medical condition, and about the possibility that she may injure herself again because of that condition. Given what has transpired, it is necessary that I explain the university's limited ability to monitor a situation such as this. Residents of university housing are adults, and the university does not monitor the day-to-day activities of residents. While we are concerned about Student's well-being, the university is not responsible for protecting your daughter from her own self-destructive tendencies.

NEW DIRECTIONS FOR STUDENT SERVICES, no. 122, Summer 2008 © Wiley Periodicals, Inc.
Published online in Wiley InterScience (www.interscience.wiley.com) • DOI: 10.1002/ss.279

Prior to this incident, your daughter had not communicated to residence hall staff members regarding her medical condition. Any information you can provide to the Office of the Vice President for Student Services about Student's medical status would be helpful. Specifically, I would like to know of her medical diagnosis, of any previous attempts of self-destructive behavior, and of any medical drugs that have been prescribed. If you have information to share with me, I would appreciate it in written form.

For students in need of psychological counseling, the university maintains a staff of professional psychologists. The University Counseling Center is located in Brick Hall, phone number XXX-XXX-XXXX. Psychological counseling at the center is offered free of charge to students. If Student is in need of psychiatric care, she may schedule an appointment with one of the two staff psychiatrists at Student Health Services.

Because participation in counseling programs is medical record information protected by federal and state law, the university cannot legally disclose to you counseling information without the written permission of your daughter. For these reasons, I recommend that you verify that Student is participating in a counseling program by asking Student to sign a release of information waiver to you when she meets with her doctor and/or counselor.

In the process of assisting Student, university staff members discovered a note that she had written shortly before the attempted suicide. While the content of the note is unsettling, I believe that you as her parents should have the copy that is enclosed.

Student may choose to withdraw from her fall semester courses by contacting the university registrar in Old Stony Hall (Room 1). If you are considering a withdrawal and have questions about the process for withdrawal, speak with Ms. Smith, the Associate Dean of Students, at XXX-XXX-XXXX. *Under University policy, only the student can effectuate a withdrawal. If the student declines to fill out a withdrawal card at the registrar's office, the student will remain officially enrolled.*

It is unfortunate that I must communicate with you under these circumstances. If you have any questions about university policies or services, feel free to contact me at XXX-XXX-XXXX. If I am not available, please speak with the associate dean of students.

Sincerely,

Vice President for Student Services
and Dean of Students

Enclosure
cc: University Counseling Center
     Student Health Services
     Residence Hall Coordinator
     Student X

Sample Health and Safety Letter for Alcohol Intoxication Requiring Hospitalization

March 4, 2008

Mr. and Mrs. X
101 Parent Drive
Some Town, USA 00000

Dear Mr. and Mrs. X:

I am writing to inform you that your son, Student, was arrested for public intoxication and taken to University Hospitals & Clinics on November 31. It is the policy of the Student Services Office to notify a student's parents in cases such as this where the student's health or safety appeared to be seriously threatened on campus as a result of self-destructive behavior. In order to ensure you are aware of this serious situation, the facts known to the Office of the Vice President for Student Services are provided below.

[Insert details of the incident here.]

Because he put himself at risk by drinking too much alcohol and was guilty of public intoxication, Student was placed on disciplinary probation. If he were to violate university conduct rules on a subsequent occasion during the academic year, Student would more than likely be suspended from the university for a minimum of one semester. Student agreed to complete a substance abuse education program at Student Health Services as soon as possible.

I am concerned about the circumstances surrounding Student's arrest and involuntary hospitalization. If a similar incident were to occur in the future, staff members might not be able to intervene in time to protect Student from the consequences of his own self-destructive behavior. The university does not monitor the activities of students and does not have the legal authority to prevent students from leaving campus and engaging in dangerous self-destructive behavior on non-university property. In order to discourage underage consumption of alcohol by students on non-university property, the university has formed a community partnership with the city council and local law enforcement agencies.

I recommend that Student observe state laws prohibiting underage drinking. I also recommend that he complete all necessary substance abuse classes as soon as possible. Because participation in counseling programs is medical record information protected by federal and state law, the university cannot legally disclose to you counseling information without the written permission of your son. For these reasons, I recommend that you verify Student's participation in the substance abuse program by asking Student to sign a release of information waiver to you when he meets with the counselor.

NEW DIRECTIONS FOR STUDENT SERVICES • DOI: 10.1002/ss

It is unfortunate that I must communicate with you under these circumstances. If you have any questions about university policies or services, or if you have any information to offer that may assist us in counseling your son, feel free to contact me at XXX-XXX-XXXX. If I am not available, please speak with the Associate Dean of Students.

Sincerely,

Vice President for Student Services
and Dean of Students

cc: Hall Manager
     Student Health
     Student X

NEW DIRECTIONS FOR STUDENT SERVICES • DOI: 10.1002/ss

Sample Letter to Parents of Minor Students

March 4, 2008

Mr. and Mrs. X
101 Parent Drive
Some Town, USA 00000

Re: University Policies Affecting Minors

Dear Mr. and Mrs. X:

Each year, a small percentage of new students enrolled at the university are not yet 18 years of age at the time classes begin. It is my understanding that your Student will turn 18 years of age after the date of enrollment. The purpose of this letter is to inform you about important health and safety policies affecting minors. Most university policies apply equally to adult-age students and to students under the age of 18. However, for certain issues—such as medical record information—university policies differentiate between minors and adults.

During the admission process, the university does not distinguish between applicants based on age. Depending on high school performance and test scores, a student may be admitted to the university even though he or she will not reach the age of majority (18) by the start of enrollment. A similar policy is followed with regard to on-campus housing. A minor eligible to enroll at the university who applies for on-campus housing is assigned a room just as an 18-year-old first-year student would be assigned a room. Students living in the residence halls are expected to be mature enough to live independently without supervision. The activities of college students, including minor students, are not monitored. The university housing system is not designed to provide special supervision for students under the age of 18.

Parents are advised to find alternative housing if they believe their son or daughter is not mature enough to live independently in an environment where building access is not restricted to residents only and the residents are free to come and go as they please. If you have any questions about residence halls policies, please call University Housing's Contracts and Assignments Office at XXX-XXX-XXXX. To cancel a housing contract prior to move-in, notice of cancellation must be made in writing to the University Housing Office in Residence Hall. While the university is responsible for operating safe housing facilities, the university and the state do not compensate students and family members when a student suffers an injury or property loss as a result of the student's negligence.

Once enrolled, a student under 18 years of age has the same general rights to education record confidentiality as adult-age students. I usually advise parents to communicate directly with their children about academic progress, disciplinary status, and other important matters. A young college student is more likely to succeed academically if parents follow the student's progress and provide input and guidance. In order to facilitate parent monitoring of academic progress, the university online ISIS registration system has been designed to enable students to assign a password to permit parent access to semester course grades. Because federal education records law treats college students under the age of 18 the same as adult students, your Student will have to provide you with a password in order for you to view his or her grades on the Internet.

Other student information such as class schedule and U-bill charges can be made available to the parents by the student through ISIS. Once a student registers for courses, he or she may elect to have the university billing statement mailed to a designated parent address through the ISIS student information system. If you don't have Web access and prefer a paper copy of the grades, your Student can print out the grades for you using ISIS. In emergency situations, or in cases where a student violates residence hall alcohol or drug rules, the university will disclose confidential education information to parents with or without the permission of the student.

University policy permits all students 18 and over to use their UI student card to charge for goods and services at the university bookstore, union food service, and at other on-campus business locations. All charges are placed on the student's U-bill. For ID cardholders under 18 years of age to charge, written parental authorization is necessary before charging is permitted. To obtain an ID charge release form, please complete and return the authorization form located at [www.Web Address.edu]. This form should be returned to the [office mailing address]. If you choose not to sign the release form, your student will not be eligible to charge for goods and services until he or she turns 18 years of age.

The university policy on medical records does differentiate between minor students and adult students. Emergency medical care is provided to all students regardless of age, but parental consent is required for many forms of nonemergency services if the student is not yet 18 years of age. Parental permission is required for vaccinations, for example. A student not yet 18 years of age also needs parental consent in order to obtain certain counseling and therapy services on campus. Once the student turns 18, parental consent is no longer required for health and counseling services, and prior written consent from the student is a prerequisite to disclosing medical record information to parents.

Because medical records laws do not distinguish between minors who are living independently while attending college and those who are still living with their parents, I am enclosing a Student Health Service consent form for you to consider. If you prefer to authorize all forms of medical care at the Student Health Service, please complete the attached document and return it to the Student Health Service. If you wish to authorize counseling services to your minor student in addition to medical services, parental consent forms are available at the University Counseling Service (XXX-XXX-XXXX).

The university firmly believes that a healthy student-parent relationship is important to the student's complete educational development. If your Student has special medical or counseling needs, we recommend that he or she sign a medical information release form during the initial meeting with the university physician or counselor.

Sincerely,

Associate Dean of Students

University Policy on Disclosing Student Record Information to Parents

Orientation Program for Parents: 2007–08 Academic Year
A healthy student-parent relationship is important to the student's complete educational development. Young college students are more likely to succeed academically if they communicate regularly with parents, and if parents provide timely guidance as they follow the student's progress. Student-parent communication is particularly important in those cases where the student encounters academic difficulties or receives sanctions for nonacademic infractions.

Federal law and state law regulate the disclosure of college student record information and medical records of persons 18 and older. There are exceptions in the law that the University routinely uses to ensure that parents receive the following information:

- Final Grades, Billing Charges, Class Schedule, and other important academic information is made available on the internet through the university student information system ISIS once a guest account is created for you by your student. The creation and maintenance of a guest account for you is completely under the control of your student. U-bills will be sent to the address selected by the student.
- Health Emergencies. If a student living in University residence halls is taken to the hospital following an episode of self-destructive behavior, the Vice President for Student Services ordinarily writes to the student's parents in order to disclose nonmedical information about the circumstances of the trip to the hospital.
- Residence Hall Alcohol and Drug Sanctions. Parents are notified in writing by the Vice President for Student Services of sanctions imposed on students for violating the residence hall alcohol policy or the residence hall drug policy.

Medical records of persons 18 and older are strictly confidential and not accessible by central administration. After a student undergoes medical care or receives psychological counseling, the health records are maintained by the service provider in medical files separate from the student's academic records. If your son or daughter has special medical or counseling needs (including substance abuse counseling), and if you wish information about these visits, the University recommends that you verify his or her attendance by asking your son or daughter to sign a release of information waiver to you when he or she meets with the physician or counselor.

In conversation with the son or daughter, parents may learn of events that took place outside of the residence halls and outside of the classroom. Parents interested in obtaining nonacademic information about police

NEW DIRECTIONS FOR STUDENT SERVICES • DOI: 10.1002/ss

arrests, disciplinary actions, or other nonmedical information are encouraged to contact the Office of the Vice President for Student Services and ask for a nonacademic information release form. When an information release form signed by the student has been received by the Vice President following an incident, information on file in the Vice President's office will be disclosed in a timely manner to all individuals named in the release. For information about off-campus criminal charges, the best resource for current information is the State Courts Online Search web site at *[www.Web Address.gov]*.

Except for final grade records, which are centralized in the Office of the Registrar, information about a student's status in a particular course is maintained by the course instructor. Consistent with federal and state law, course instructors do not release information to persons outside of the university, including parents. Even when a student is not yet 18, federal and state law requires a written information release signed by the student to disclose collegiate academic records. If your student creates an ISIS guest account for you that grants you permission to view the information presented on the ISIS guest access screens, additional education record information cannot be disclosed to you without the written consent of your student.

If you have questions about the University records policy as it relates to parental notification, contact the Associate Dean of Students at *[mailing address, phone number, and e-mail address]*.

INDEX